THE HEALTHY KIDS COOKBOOK

Prize-Winning Recipes for Sliders, Chili, Tots, Salads, and More for Every Family

Skyhorse Pubishing

Source: U.S. Department of Agriculture.

First Skyhorse Publishing edition 2019. All rights to any and all materials in copyright owned by the publisher are strictly reserved by the publisher. All inquiries should be addressed to Skyhorse Publishing, 307 West 36th Street, 11th Floor, New York, NY 10018.

Skyhorse Publishing books may be purchased in bulk at special discounts for sales promotion, corporate gifts, fund-raising, or educational purposes. Special editions can also be created to specifications. For details, contact the Special Sales Department, Skyhorse Publishing, 307 West 36th Street, 11th Floor, New York, NY 10018 or info@skyhorsepublishing.com.

Skyhorse® and Skyhorse Publishing® are registered trademarks of Skyhorse Publishing, Inc.®, a Delaware corporation.

Visit our website at www.skyhorsepublishing.com.

10 9 8 7 6 5 4 3 2 1

Library of Congress Cataloging-in-Publication Data is available on file.

Print ISBN: 978-1-5107-5074-6
eBook: 978-1-5107-5079-1

Cover design by Daniel Brount

Printed in China

Table of Contents

8 Porcupine Sliders
Grand Prize Winner

30 Tasty Tots
Popular Choice Winner

58 Tuscan Smoked Turkey and Bean Soup
1st Place Winner

Recipes for Healthy Kids Competition Acknowledgement Page

The United States Department of Agriculture (USDA), Food and Nutrition Service (FNS) would like to thank the following people and organizations for their support of the *Recipes for Healthy Kids* Competition. The *Recipes for Healthy Kids* Competition provided the perfect opportunity for school nutrition professionals, students, parents, chefs, and community members to cook up some new ideas and get children excited about making healthy choices. We want to thank all of the *Recipes for Healthy Kids* teams that participated in the competition. The teams submitted over 340 recipes for this contest.

United States Department of Agriculture

Food and Nutrition Service, USDA

Project Lead
Ann Hall, MRE, RD, LDN

Project Team

Eileen Ferruggiaro, PhD, RD	Erika Pijai, MS, RD
Tim Vazquez, RD	Julie Fort, MPH, RD
Heidi Bishop	Desiré Stapley, MEd, RD
Sonya Barnes, MS, RD	Natalie Partridge, MS, RD
Sheldon Gordon, MS, RD	Bruce Alexander
Mydina Thabet, MS, RD, LDN	Cheryl Wilson
Ebony S. James, MS, RD	Jack Currie
Michelle Prettyman, RD, LD	Mary Jean Kirchner
Barbara Jirka, PhD, SNS	Sherl White
Gwen Holcomb	Tama Eliff
Cheryl Jackson Lewis, MPA, RD, LDN	Angela Leone, MS, RD

Challenge Post

Administered the contest and designed and monitored Web site
Brandon Kessler
Samantha Tse
Colin Nederkoorn

School Nutrition Association (SNA)

Each school day, SNA members take on the challenge of serving healthy, nutritious meals to more than 31 million school children.

Judges
Katie Wilson, PhD, SNS
Helen E. Phillips, SNS
Karen M. Green

American Culinary Federation (ACF)

One of their many roles includes serving as the official representative for the Chef & Child Foundation, founded in 1989, to educate children and families in understanding proper nutrition and serving as the voice of the culinary industry in its fight against childhood hunger, malnutrition, and obesity.

ACF National President
Michael Ty, CEC, AAC

ACF Government Relations Committee Chair
Damian Martineau, AAC

Judges
Shawn L. Hanlin, CEC
Rene J. Marquis, CEC, CCE, PCEC, CCA, AAC
Roland E. Schaeffer, CEC, AAC, HOF
Randy J. Torres, CEC
David J. Turcotte, CEC, AAC

ACF Staff
Heidi Cramb
Kevin Brune
Patricia A. Carroll
Tracy Smith
Michelle Whitfield, MHA

Roniece Weaver & Associates, Inc. (RWA)

RWA is an Orlando-based consulting nutrition practice, headed by Roniece Weaver, MS, RD, LD. The focus is on integrating food, wellness, and innovative cooking strategies. RWA was responsible for testing, evaluation, and recipe standardization.

Hebni Nutrition Consultants	Fabiola Gaines
Glen R. Providence	Candace Weaver
Larry Walker	Gloria Jolly
Don Carlock	Ellareetha Carson
Bridget Monroe	Rojean Williams
Yolanda Daniels	Charles Daniels
Keon Johnson	Dr. Maurice Woodard
Anthony McCastler	

Holly Graphics
Design and layout by Byron Holly

Mark Taulbee Photography
Photographs

Food Safety Advice

Clean: Wash Hands and Surfaces Often

Bacteria can be spread throughout the kitchen and get onto hands, cutting boards, utensils, counter tops, and food.

■ Wash your hands with warm water and soap for at least 20 seconds before and after handling food and after using the bathroom or changing diapers.

■ Wash your cutting boards, dishes, utensils, and counter tops with hot soapy water, or prepare your sanitizer according to the manufacturer's instructions, before you go on to the next food.

■ Consider using paper towels to clean up kitchen surfaces. If you use cloth towels wash them often in the hot cycle of your washing machine.

■ Rinse fresh fruits and vegetables under running tap water, including those with skins and rinds that are not eaten.

■ Rub firm-skinned fruits and vegetables under running tap water or scrub with a clean vegetable brush while rinsing with running tap water.

■ Keep books, backpacks, or shopping bags off the kitchen table or counters where food is prepared or served.

Separate: Don't Cross Contaminate

Cross-contamination is how bacteria can be spread. When handling raw meat, poultry, seafood, and eggs, keep these foods and their juices away from ready-to-eat foods.

■ Separate raw meat, poultry, seafood, and eggs from other foods in your grocery shopping cart, grocery bags, and in your refrigerator.

■ Use one cutting board for fresh produce and a separate one for raw meat, poultry, and seafood.

■ Never place cooked food on a plate that previously held raw meat, poultry, seafood, or eggs.

Cook: Cook to Proper Temperatures

Food is safely cooked when it reaches a high enough internal temperature to kill the harmful bacteria that cause foodborne illness. Use a food thermometer to measure the internal temperature of cooked foods.

■ Use a food thermometer, which measures the internal temperature of cooked meat, poultry, and egg dishes, to make sure that the food is cooked to a safe internal temperature.

■ Make sure there are no cold spots in food (where bacteria can survive) when cooking in a microwave oven. For best results, cover food, stir, and rotate for even cooking. If there is no turntable, rotate the dish by hand once or twice during cooking.

■ Use microwave-safe cookware and plastic wrap when cooking foods in a microwave oven.

Chill: Refrigerate Promptly!

Refrigerate foods quickly because cold temperatures slow the growth of harmful bacteria. Do not over-stuff the refrigerator. Cold air must circulate to help keep food safe. Keeping a constant refrigerator temperature of 40 °F or below is one of the most effective ways to reduce the risk of foodborne illness. Use an appliance thermometer to be sure the temperature is consistently 40 °F or below. The freezer temperature should be 0 °F or below.

■ Refrigerate or freeze meat, poultry, eggs, and other perishables as soon as you get them home from the store.
■ Never let raw meat, poultry, eggs, cooked food, or cut fresh fruits or vegetables sit at room temperature more than two hours before putting them in the refrigerator or freezer (one hour when the temperature is above 90 °F).
■ There are three safe ways to defrost food: in the refrigerator, in cold water, and in the microwave using the defrost setting. Food thawed in cold water or in the microwave should be cooked immediately.
■ Always marinate food in the refrigerator.
■ Use or discard refrigerated food on a regular basis.

Keeping Cold Lunches Cold

Prepare cooked food, such as turkey, ham, chicken, and vegetable or pasta salads, ahead of time to allow for

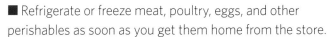

thorough chilling in the refrigerator. Keep cooked food refrigerated until time to leave home.

To keep lunches cold away from home, include a small frozen gel pack or frozen juice box. If there's a refrigerator available, store perishable items there upon arrival. Insulated, soft-sided lunch boxes or bags are best for keeping food cold, but metal or plastic lunch boxes and paper bags can also be used. If using paper lunch bags, create layers by double bagging to help insulate the food.

Some food is safe without a cold source. Items that don't require refrigeration include whole fruits and vegetables, hard cheese, unopened canned meat and fish, chips, breads, crackers, peanut butter, jelly, mustard, and pickles.

Keeping Hot Lunches Hot

Use an insulated container to keep food like soup, chili, and stew hot. Fill the container with boiling water, let stand for a few minutes, empty, and then put in the piping hot food. Keep the insulated container closed until lunchtime to keep the food hot — 140 °F or above.

For more information, visit the USDA Food Safety and Inspection Service (FSIS): fsis.usda.gov

Recipes for Healthy Kids Cookbook

Kid-Approved Recipes For Home

If you're looking to add to your collection of delicious, kid-approved recipes that are made from healthy ingredients, look no further than the *Recipes for Healthy Kids Cookbook*. The recipes in this cookbook feature foods that children and adults alike should consume more of: dark green and orange vegetables, dry beans and peas, and whole grains. All of these healthy recipes are low in total fat, saturated fat, sugar, and sodium. With fun names such as Porcupine Sliders, Smokin' Powerhouse Chili, and Squish Squash Lasagna, even picky eaters are sure to taste and try these recipes. The featured recipes serve six, include no more than 15 commonly available ingredients, and are easy for families and home child care providers to prepare. These kid-tested, kid-approved recipes are sure to please children and be an instant hit at home or in your home child care program!

This cookbook features a collection of recipes from the *Recipes for Healthy Kids Competition*. The top recipes in each category have been standardized for cookbooks for home, child care centers, and schools. The cookbooks and recipes are also available from the Team Nutrition Web site at TeamNutrition.usda.gov.

The Challenge From the White House

This cookbook contains the top 30 recipes from the *Recipes for Healthy Kids Competition*, which the U.S. Department of Agriculture (USDA) launched in September 2010. The USDA collaborated with the American Culinary Federation (ACF) and the School Nutrition Association (SNA) on this nationwide competition. Teams of students (grades 4 to 12), school nutrition professionals, chefs, parents, and other interested community members were challenged to partner and create tasty and healthy new recipes. The recipe challenge was created to increase students' intake of foods in these under-consumed competition categories: dark green and orange vegetables, dry beans and peas, and whole grains.

Each "Recipe Challenge Team" used the talents of its team members to create recipes that could be a new creation or a twist on a recipe already being enjoyed at the school. Chefs provided food expertise, while school nutrition professionals shared insight as to what can be accomplished in school settings. Together the chef and school nutrition professional assisted kids, parents, and community members to prepare nutritious dishes which students would actually choose. Each team held taste-testing events at its school to help ensure their recipes would be a winner at the competition.

The Recipes for Healthy Kids Competition

After weeks of hard work by the teams, over 340 recipes were submitted to the competition. What followed was an extensive process of reviewing, ranking, and judging. The top three schools with the winning recipe from each category prepared their dish at a national cook-off.

■ **Reviewing and ranking:** The 340 eligible recipes were reviewed and ranked within each category by teams of ACF chefs and USDA Food and Nutrition Service (FNS) staff to determine the top 30 recipes, 10 in each of the three recipe categories.

■ **Onsite judging:** The top 15 teams were visited by a team of three judges, made up of an FNS staff member, an ACF chef, and a school nutrition professional. The

judges were met with a warm welcome and much enthusiasm by the recipe challenge teams at each school. The recipes were served to the students. The judges sampled and scored each recipe and chose the First Place Finalist in each category.

■ **National cook-off:** The three First Place Finalists competed in a national Cook-off held at the ACF National Convention in July 2011. Competing for the Grand Prize were the teams preparing Porcupine Sliders, Central Valley Harvest Bake, and Tuscan Smoked Turkey and Bean Soup. Judges included President of the School Nutrition Association, Helen Phillips and two ACF chefs, Rene Marquis and Shawn Hanlin. Porcupine Sliders was the Grand Prize winner of the Recipes for Healthy Kids Competition.

■ **Public Choice voting:** In addition to the national cook-off, over 16,000 public votes were cast online to determine the Popular Choice winner from the top 15 semi-finalist recipes at the competition's Web site. The winning recipe, Tasty Tots, received over 2,000 community votes.

Winning Recipes

The top recipes in each category were judged on student involvement, nutrition, creativity and originality, ease of use in schools, and recipe presentation. A total of $12,000 in prizes was given to the recipe category winners to benefit their school meals programs.

Porcupine Sliders

SOUTH EDUCATION CENTER ALTERNATIVE SCHOOL
Richfield, Minnesota

Our Story

The South Education Center Alternative (SECA) School recipe challenge team put their heads together in the school kitchen, mixing and matching the ingredients to find the perfect blend and created the national cook-off Grand Prize winning Porcupine Sliders.

What exactly are Porcupine Sliders? They are healthy, mouth-watering turkey burgers, high in protein, with just the right amount of spices and a kick of sweet cranberries, all served on small whole-wheat rolls. The addition of brown rice to the burger mixture created a prickly look like little porcupines – thus their name.

Porcupine Sliders are a delicious, nutritious, and appetizing new way to get kids to eat healthy. The simple ingredients and easy preparation makes them a favorable choice for a quick menu idea that kids will enjoy!

School Team Members

SCHOOL NUTRITION PROFESSIONAL: Wanda Nickolai
CHEF: Todd Bolton (Parasole Restaurant Holdings, Inc.)
COMMUNITY MEMBERS: Theresa Guthrie (Family and Consumer Science Teacher) and Mary Lair (School Nurse, Bloomington Public Health)
STUDENTS: Adilene D., Chris D., Dominic L., and Dolores P.

GRAND PRIZE WINNER
Recipes for Healthy Kids

These mouth-watering turkey burgers are made with the right amount of spices and a burst of sweet cranberries and served on small whole-wheat rolls; watch children delight in the flavors!

Porcupine Sliders

Ingredients

⅛ cup Brown rice, long-grain, regular, dry

1 tsp Canola oil

1 ½ Tbsp Fresh onion, peeled, diced

¼ cup Fresh celery, diced

1 ½ tsp Fresh garlic, minced

1 lb Raw ground turkey, lean

1 Egg, beaten

5 Tbsp Dried cranberries, chopped

¾ cup Fresh baby spinach, chopped

1 tsp Worcestershire sauce

½ tsp Salt

½ tsp Ground black pepper

1 dash Ground white pepper

6 (1 oz each) Mini whole-wheat rolls (small dinner roll size)

Preparation Time: 30 minutes
Cooking Time: 1 hour 20 minutes
Makes six sliders
1 slider provides 2 oz equivalent meat/meat alternate and 1 oz equivalent grains.

Directions

1. Preheat oven to 350 °F.

2. Combine brown rice and ½ cup water in a small pot and bring to a boil. Turn heat down to low. Cover and cook until water is absorbed, about 30-40 minutes. Fluff with a fork. Cover and refrigerate until completely cooled. A rice cooker may be used with the same quantity of brown rice and water.

3. Heat canola oil in a small skillet. Add onions, celery, and garlic. Cook over medium heat for 5 minutes or until tender. Remove from heat. Cover and refrigerate until completely cooled.

4. In a medium mixing bowl, combine turkey, egg, cranberries, spinach, Worcestershire sauce, salt, peppers, brown rice, and sautéed vegetables. Mix well. Shape into 6 patties.

5. Line a large baking sheet with parchment paper and lightly coat with nonstick cooking spray. Place patties evenly spaced on baking sheet.

6. Bake uncovered for 20-25 minutes at 350 °F to an internal temperature of 165 °F or higher for at least 15 seconds (use a food thermometer to check the internal temperature). Do not overcook. Remove from oven and serve on a mini whole-wheat roll. Serve immediately.

7. May be served with onion, lettuce, tomatoes, ketchup, and mustard.

Nutrients Per Serving: Calories **247**, Protein **16 g**, Carbohydrate **26 g**, Dietary Fiber **3 g**, Total Fat **9 g**, Saturated Fat **2 g**, Cholesterol **85 mg**, Vitamin A **540 IU (41 RAE)**, Vitamin C **2 mg**, Iron **2 mg**, Calcium **65 mg**, Sodium **366 mg**

Chic' Penne

WINOGRAD K-8 ELEMENTARY SCHOOL
Greeley, Colorado

Our Story

The Winograd K-8 Elementary School team started the recipe creation discussing all the foods eligible for the competition. Then, they wrote down what each team member liked to eat. After a couple of test runs of basic dishes, they ended up with a tasty dish called Chic' Penne.

Not found at your local fast food restaurant, Chic' Penne has a little hint of black pepper and is anything but ordinary. By combining the best ingredients, this recipe produces a dish that not only looks good, but tastes good too! This main dish will be an instant hit with your children.

School Team Members

SCHOOL NUTRITION PROFESSIONAL: Kara Sample, RD, SNS
CHEF: Amanda Smith
COMMUNITY MEMBER: Emily Wigington (AmeriCorps VISTA Volunteer)
STUDENTS: Jace K., Bethany V., Abraham A., and Amairani P.

1ST PLACE WINNER
Whole Grains

This whole-wheat pasta dish is bright and fun with fresh broccoli, chicken, and melted cheese that is sure to please.

Chic' Penne

Ingredients

3 cups Penne pasta, whole-wheat, dry (12 oz)

1 tsp Granulated garlic

2 cups Fresh broccoli florets

1 cup Cooked diced chicken, ½" pieces (4 oz)

1 ½ cups Fat-free half and half

1 Tbsp Enriched all-purpose flour

⅛ cup Low-sodium chicken broth

1 tsp Salt

½ tsp Ground black pepper

½ cup Reduced-fat cheddar cheese, shredded (2 oz)

½ cup Low-fat mozzarella cheese, low-moisture, part-skim, shredded (2 oz)

Preparation Time: 20 minutes
Cooking Time: 20 minutes
Makes six 1 ½-cup servings

1 ½ cups provides 1 oz equivalent meat/meat alternate, ⅛ cup vegetable, and 1 ¾ oz equivalent grains.

Directions

1. Preheat oven to 350 °F.

2. In a large pot, bring 2 quarts water to a boil. Gradually stir in pasta and return to a boil. Cook uncovered for 8-10 minutes or until tender. Do not overcook. Drain well. Toss pasta with ½ teaspoon garlic.

3. Fill a medium pot with water and bring to a boil. Add broccoli florets and cook for 5 minutes. Drain well. Sprinkle with remaining garlic.

4. Transfer pasta and broccoli to a medium casserole dish (about 8" x 11") coated with nonstick cooking spray. Add chicken. Mix well.

5. In a small mixing bowl, mix ½ cup half and half with flour. Whisk to remove lumps.

6. In a medium skillet, heat chicken broth, salt, pepper, and remaining half and half. Stir constantly. Stir in half and half/flour mixture. Stir constantly and bring to a boil.

7. Reduce heat to low. Stir frequently for 5 minutes. Sauce will thicken. Add cheese and stir until cheese melts. Remove from heat. Pour sauce over broccoli/pasta mixture.

8. Cover casserole dish with lid or with foil. Bake at 350 °F for 8 minutes. Heat to an internal temperature of 165 °F or higher for at least 15 seconds (use a food thermometer to check the internal temperature). Remove from oven. Serve hot.

Nutrients Per Serving: Calories **300**, Protein **19 g**, Carbohydrate **44 g**, Dietary Fiber **6 g**, Total Fat **6 g**, Saturated Fat **2 g**, Cholesterol **26 mg**, Vitamin A **618 IU (78 RAE)**, Vitamin C **17 mg**, Iron **2 mg**, Calcium **231 mg**, Sodium **418 mg**

Mediterranean Quinoa Salad

BELLINGHAM MEMORIAL MIDDLE SCHOOL
Bellingham, Massachusetts

Our Story

Bellingham Memorial Middle School in Bellingham, Massachusetts, serves over 800 students in grades 5-8. The school seeks to establish itself as an exemplary middle school by developing programs that are responsive to student needs.

The recipe challenge team held an afterschool cooking class. After a discussion on the value of healthy eating and a lesson on basic nutrition, the students went to work to create a recipe. The end result was a tasty side salad featuring a nutritious whole grain called quinoa, mixed with a colorful variety of vegetables, including red peppers, parsley, and cherry tomatoes. Feta cheese and a light lemon dressing complete the Mediterranean Quinoa Salad. What a party of flavor!

School Team Members

SCHOOL NUTRITION PROFESSIONAL: Jeanne Sheridan, SNS
CHEF: Rodney Poles (Whole Foods Market, partner chef from *Chefs Move to Schools* chefsmovetoschools.org)
COMMUNITY MEMBERS: Karen Ring (Healthy Eating Specialist, Whole Foods Market) and Lauren Marciszyn, RD, LDN (Youth and Community Wellness Director, YMCA)
STUDENTS: Dylan B., Elizabeth B., Taylin S., John G., and Nick D.

Mediterranean Quinoa Salad

Ingredients

1 cup Quinoa, dry

2 cups Low-sodium chicken broth

2 Tbsp Lemon juice

2 Tbsp Red wine vinegar

1 tsp Fresh garlic, minced

1 ½ Tbsp Extra virgin olive oil

½ tsp Salt

⅛ tsp Ground white pepper

¼ cup Fresh red bell peppers, seeded, diced

2 Tbsp Fresh green onions, diced

2 Tbsp Fresh red onions, peeled, diced

½ cup Fresh cherry tomatoes, halved

2 Tbsp Black olives, sliced

2 Tbsp Feta cheese, crumbled

1 Tbsp Fresh parsley, chopped

Preparation Time: 1 hour
Cooking Time: 10-15 minutes
Makes six ¾-cup servings

Directions

1. Rinse quinoa in a fine mesh strainer until water runs clear, not cloudy. Combine quinoa and chicken broth in a small pot. Cover and bring to a boil. Turn heat down to low and simmer until broth is completely absorbed, about 10-15 minutes. When done, quinoa will be soft and a white ring will pop out of the kernel. The white ring will appear only when it is fully cooked. Fluff with a fork. A rice cooker may be used with the same quantity of quinoa and water. Cover and refrigerate.

2. In a small mixing bowl, combine lemon juice, vinegar, garlic, olive oil, salt, and ground pepper to make dressing.

3. Combine red peppers, green onions, red onions, tomatoes, and olives in a large mixing bowl. Mix well.

4. Add dressing to vegetable mixture. Mix in cooled quinoa. Fold in feta cheese and parsley. Cover and refrigerate for about 2 hours. Serve chilled.

¾ cup provides ⅛ cup vegetable and 1 oz equivalent grains.

Nutrients Per Serving: Calories **166,** Protein **7 g,** Carbohydrate **23 g,** Dietary Fiber **3 g,** Total Fat **6 g,** Saturated Fat **1 g,** Cholesterol **3 mg,** Vitamin A **414 IU (24 RAE),** Vitamin C **12 mg,** Iron **2 mg,** Calcium **42 mg,** Sodium **278 mg**

Aztec Grain Salad

NOVI MEADOWS 6TH GRADE UPPER ELEMENTARY SCHOOL
Novi, Michigan

Our Story

Novi Meadows, an upper elementary Blue Ribbon Exemplary School, drew on the talents and hard work of students, staff, parents, and the community to create their unique recipe. The school's School Nutrition Action Committee (SNAC) brainstormed recipe ideas that would not only fulfill the nutritional requirements of the contest, but would also be appealing to the students. The SNAC wanted to come up with something that was different and chose quinoa as the whole grain to feature in the recipe. Quinoa was then paired with traditional American fall produce to create a unique flavor experience. Aztec Grain Salad was named by the students, and it is a fantastic side dish to offer children.

School Team Members

SCHOOL NUTRITION PROFESSIONAL: JoAnn Clements
CHEF: Ina Cheatem (Natural Food Chef, Fresh Delights)
COMMUNITY MEMBER: Michelle Thompson
STUDENTS: Cory G., Bryan T., and Jackie D.

Whole Grains

Aztec Grain Salad combines a South American, high-protein grain called quinoa with aromatic roasted butternut squash, crisp apples, and dried cranberries to make a delicious and colorful side dish.

Ingredients

1 ½ cups Quinoa, dry

1 ¾ cups Fresh granny smith apples, peeled, cored, cubed ¾"

1 ¾ cups Fresh butternut squash, peeled, seeded, cubed ½"

1 Tbsp Canola oil

¼ tsp Ground ginger

¾ tsp Ground cinnamon

¼ cup Frozen orange juice concentrate

1 ½ Tbsp Extra virgin olive oil

1 tsp Honey

⅓ tsp Dijon mustard

2 Tbsp Red wine vinegar

⅛ tsp Salt

1 dash Ground black pepper

1 dash Ground white pepper

½ tsp Fresh cilantro, chopped

Optional: use additional cilantro as a garnish

⅓ cup Dried cranberries, finely chopped

⅓ cup Golden raisins, seedless, finely chopped

Preparation Time: 15 minutes
Cooking Time: 30 minutes
Makes six 1-cup servings

Directions

1. Preheat oven to 400 °F.

2. Rinse quinoa in a fine mesh strainer until water runs clear, not cloudy. Combine quinoa and 3 cups water in a medium pot. Cover and bring to a boil. Turn heat down to low and simmer until water is completely absorbed, about 10-15 minutes. When done, quinoa will be soft and a white ring will pop out of the kernel. The white ring will appear only when it is fully cooked. Fluff with a fork. Cover and refrigerate. A rice cooker may be used with the same quantity of quinoa and water.

3. Combine apples and squash in a large mixing bowl. Add canola oil, ⅛ tsp ginger, and ¼ tsp cinnamon. Toss well to coat.

4. Pour apples/squash mixture onto a large baking sheet and place in oven at 400 °F. Roast for 15 minutes or until squash is soft and slightly brown on the edges. Do not overcook. Remove and set aside to cool.

5. In a medium mixing bowl, combine orange juice, olive oil, honey, Dijon mustard, red wine vinegar, salt, peppers, cilantro, and remaining ginger and cinnamon. Whisk together to make dressing.

Nutrients Per Serving: Calories **298,** Protein **6 g,** Carbohydrate **54 g,** Dietary Fiber **6 g,** Total Fat **8 g,** Saturated Fat **1 g,** Cholesterol **0 mg,** Vitamin A **3392 IU (171 RAE),** Vitamin C **15 mg,** Iron **2 mg,** Calcium **44 mg,** Sodium **58 mg**

Directions Aztec Grain Salad (continued)

6. In a large mixing bowl, combine quinoa, apples/squash mix, cranberries, raisins, and dressing. Toss well to combine. If desired, garnish with additional cilantro. Cover and refrigerate for about 2 hours. Serve chilled.

---

1 cup provides ⅛ cup vegetable, ⅜ cup fruit, and 1 oz equivalent grains.

From 10-Tips Nutrition Education Series

1. Make simple switches
To make half your grains whole grains, substitute a whole-grain product for a refined-grain product. For example, eat 100% whole-wheat bread or bagels instead of white bread or bagels, or brown rice instead of white rice.

2. Save some time
Cook extra bulgur or barley when you have time. Freeze half to heat and serve later as a quick side dish.

3. Be a smart shopper
The color of a food is not an indication that it is a whole-grain food. Foods labeled as "multi-grain," "stone-ground," "100% wheat," "cracked wheat," "seven-grain," or "bran" are usually not 100% whole-grain products, and may not contain any whole grain.

choosemyplate.gov/healthy-eating-tips/ten-tips.html

Chicken Alfredo With a Twist

VAN BUREN MIDDLE SCHOOL
Kettering, Ohio

Our Story

Located in southwest Ohio, Van Buren Middle School is a proud member of the Kettering City School Family. Out of the nine recipes developed for testing, two were submitted to the *Recipes for Healthy Kids* Competition, and the Chicken Alfredo With a Twist recipe proved to be a winner!

This recipe saves on fat and calories by using fat-free half and half, and boosts the fiber content by incorporating whole grains. Whole-wheat rotini noodles are used to replace traditional fettuccini noodles. These 'twists' make this a healthy alternative to the classic chicken alfredo. Pair a serving with a refreshing vegetable side dish to give your kids a meal that is sure to please!

School Team Members

SCHOOL NUTRITION PROFESSIONAL: Louise Easterly, LD, SNS
CHEF: Rachel Tilford
COMMUNITY MEMBER: Mary Kozarec (School Nurse)
STUDENTS: Graham B., Jonathan A., Shawnrica W., and Savannah S.

Whole Grains

This rich and creamy recipe gives ordinary chicken alfredo a healthy twist, combining fat-free half and half with canned cream of chicken soup and whole-wheat rotini noodles.

Chicken Alfredo With a Twist

Ingredients

2 ½ cups Rotini pasta, whole-wheat, dry (10 oz)

2 cans Low-fat, reduced-sodium cream of chicken soup (two 10¾-oz cans)

1 ⅓ cups Fat-free half and half

¼ tsp Ground white pepper

⅛ tsp Garlic powder

⅓ cup Grated parmesan cheese

3 cups Cooked diced chicken, ½″ pieces (12 oz)

Preparation Time: 15 minutes
Cooking Time: 15 minutes
Makes six 1-cup servings

Directions

1. In a large pot, bring 2 quarts water to a boil. Gradually stir in pasta and return to a boil. Cook uncovered about 8-10 minutes or until tender. Do not overcook. Drain well.

2. Mix soup, half-and-half, pepper, garlic powder, parmesan cheese, and chicken in a large pot. Cook for 5 minutes over medium heat, stirring often. Heat to 165 °F or higher for at least 15 seconds

3. Combine noodles and sauce right before serving. Serve hot.

Note: Keep noodles and sauce separate until serving time. Sauce will thicken upon standing.

1 cup provides 2 ¼ oz equivalent meat/meat alternate and 1 ¼ oz equivalent grains.

Nutrients Per Serving: Calories **345,** Protein **30 g,** Carbohydrate **41 g,** Dietary Fiber **3 g,** Total Fat **8 g,** Saturated Fat **4 g,** Cholesterol **69 mg,** Vitamin A **450 IU (29 RAE),** Vitamin C **< 1 mg ,** Iron **2 mg,** Calcium **174 mg,** Sodium **572 mg**

Chicken Curry Casserole

GARFIELD ELEMENTARY SCHOOL
Washington, District of Columbia

Our Story

The students of Garfield Elementary School were eager to accept the challenge of the *Recipes for Healthy Kids* Competition. They met to brainstorm ideas. The recipe challenge team developed three recipes which were prepared for the entire school. Based on the student reviews, the team revised the recipes and submitted them to the competition. Chicken Curry Casserole was the winner. This chicken curry recipe originated from a student who was inspired by a favorite dish her aunt makes at home. Chicken Curry Casserole is a dish to warm the heart and please the soul!

School Team Members

SCHOOL NUTRITION PROFESSIONAL: Danielle Schaub, RD (Registered Dietitian, Chartwells-Thompson)
CHEF: Clay Berry (Executive Chef, Chartwells-Thompson)
COMMUNITY MEMBER: Sapna Batheja, MS, RD (Project Manager, American Association of School Administrators)
STUDENTS: Mark K., Carmen J., and Samya C.

Whole Grains

In this traditional, spiced Indian dish, tender chicken strips, fresh carrots, diced celery, and brown rice are tossed in a creamy curry sauce and baked until golden.

20

Chicken Curry Casserole

Ingredients

1 cup Brown rice, long-grain, regular, dry

1 Tbsp Canola oil

¼ cup Low-sodium chicken broth

¾ cup Fresh celery

1 cup Fresh onions, peeled, diced

1 ¼ cups Fresh carrots, peeled, shredded

1 ½ tsp Curry powder

1 tsp Garlic powder

½ tsp Ground black pepper

¾ tsp Salt

½ cup Low-fat plain yogurt

2 cups Cooked fajita chicken strips, diced 1" (12 oz)

Preparation Time: 15 minutes
Cooking Time: 1 hour 5 minutes
Makes six ¾-cup servings

Directions

1. Preheat oven to 400 °F.

2. Combine brown rice and 2 ½ cups water in large pot and bring to a boil. Turn heat down to low. Cover and cook until water is absorbed, about 30-40 minutes. Fluff with a fork. Set aside. A rice cooker may be used with the same quantity of brown rice and water.

3. In a large pan, heat canola oil and chicken broth over medium heat for 2-3 minutes. Add celery, onions, and carrots. Cook an additional 5-7 minutes or until vegetables are tender.

4. In a large mixing bowl, combine curry powder, garlic powder, pepper, salt, and yogurt. Add vegetables, brown rice, and chicken. Mix well.

5. Pour mixture into a 9" x 9" nonstick baking pan. Bake uncovered at 400 °F for 15 minutes. Heat to an internal temperature of 165 °F or higher for at least 15 seconds (use a food thermometer to check the internal temperature). Serve hot.

¾ cup provides 1 ¼ oz equivalent meat/meat alternate, ¼ cup vegetable, and ¾ oz equivalent grains.

Nutrients Per Serving: Calories **220,** Protein **14 g,** Carbohydrate **26 g,** Dietary Fiber **3 g,** Total Fat **6 g,** Saturated Fat **1 g,** Cholesterol **51 mg,** Vitamin A **3162 IU (158 RAE),** Vitamin C **3 mg,** Iron **1 mg,** Calcium **65 mg,** Sodium **564 mg**

Oodles of Noodles

LINCOLN JUNIOR HIGH SCHOOL
Skokie, Illinois

Our Story

When the Assistant Principal asks you to work on a recipe challenge project, you roll up your sleeves and get busy! For the recipe challenge team at Lincoln Junior High School, foodservice members, teachers, students, parents, and a chef all came together to cook, taste, and adjust recipes.

They developed a total of five recipes. Thirty students were asked to comment on each recipe and share whether or not they would eat the dish if it were served again. Based on their feedback, the school submitted three recipes as part of the contest and is thrilled that one of their recipes, Oodles of Noodles, was selected.

School Team Members

SCHOOL NUTRITION PROFESSIONAL: Kathy Jones
CHEF: Patsy Bentivegna
COMMUNITY MEMBERS: Joe Cullota (Teacher) and Maggie Nessim (School Board Member and Parent)
STUDENTS: Sarah B., Matt L., Elizabeth D., Vanessa L., and Hannah W.

Whole Grains

This colorful, whole-wheat pasta dish is accented with grape tomatoes and Swiss chard, and delicately flavored with basil and garlic for an oodles of noodle delight!

Oodles of Noodles

Ingredients

2¾ cups Penne pasta, whole-wheat, dry (11 oz)

1 ½ Tbsp Extra virgin olive oil

2 ¼ cups Fresh grape tomatoes, halved

1 ½ tsp Dried basil

¾ tsp Sea salt

¼ tsp Ground black pepper

1 Tbsp Fresh garlic, minced

3 Tbsp Whole-wheat flour

2 ⅓ cups Low-sodium vegetable broth

4 cups Fresh Swiss chard, stems removed, chopped

Preparation Time: 15 minutes
Cooking Time: 20 minutes
Makes six 1-cup servings

Directions

1. In a large pot, bring 2 quarts water to a boil. Gradually stir in pasta and return to a boil. Cook uncovered for about 8-10 minutes until tender. Do not overcook. Drain well.

2. Heat olive oil in a large skillet over medium heat. Add half of tomatoes and cook 2-3 minutes until skins soften. Do not overcook. Reserve remaining tomatoes for step 4. Add basil, salt, pepper, and garlic. Stir.

3. Sprinkle flour over tomatoes. Cook for 30 seconds over medium heat until mixture becomes thick. Add vegetable broth. Bring to a boil and then immediately reduce to low heat.

4. Add Swiss chard and remaining tomatoes. Simmer uncovered over low heat for 1-2 minutes or until Swiss chard is wilted. Pour over pasta. Serve hot.

1 cup provides ¼ cup vegetable, and 2 oz equivalent grains.

Nutrients Per Serving: Calories **235,** Protein **9 g,** Carbohydrate **43 g,** Dietary Fiber **5 g,** Total Fat **4 g,** Saturated Fat **1 g,** Cholesterol **0 mg,** Vitamin A **1519 IU (76 RAE),** Vitamin C **15 mg,** Iron **5 mg,** Calcium **50 mg,** Sodium **323 mg**

Peppy Quinoa

SARTELL MIDDLE SCHOOL
Sartell, Minnesota

Our Story

The recipe challenge team at Sartell Middle School featured quinoa as its key ingredient. From South America, this versatile whole grain can be prepared in many different ways. As a light and fluffy alternative to rice or couscous, children are sure to enjoy quinoa—a nutty-flavored whole grain.

The team members all had one thing in common: a passion for serving healthy food to students. The recipes they developed were based on the suggestions of the students.

While testing Peppy Quinoa, more than 300 surveys were completed. The results were overwhelmingly positive, and the team realized that they had a winning recipe in their hands. Move over pasta, quinoa is in the house!

School Team Members

SCHOOL NUTRITION PROFESSIONAL: Janice Sweeter
CHEF: Paul Ruszat
COMMUNITY MEMBERS: Kelly Radi (Parent) and Lori Domburg (Teacher)
STUDENT: Bryan S.

Whole Grains

This surprisingly peppy side dish combines spicy green chilies, cilantro, and toasted pepitas with the nutty flavor of quinoa, giving this dish a Latino flair that will spice up any menu.

Peppy Quinoa

Ingredients

⅛ cup Pepitas/Pumpkin seeds

1 ¼ cups Quinoa, dry

1 Tbsp Low-sodium chicken base

½ cup Fresh onion, peeled, diced

½ cup Canned diced green chilies

2 ¼ tsp Fresh garlic, minced

½ cup Fresh cilantro, chopped

½ cup Fresh green onions, diced

2-4 Tbsp Fresh lime juice (optional)

Preparation Time: 15 minutes
Cooking Time: 1 hour 5 minutes
Makes six ½-cup servings

Directions

1. Preheat oven to 350 °F.

2. Toast pepitas in oven for 10 minutes or until light brown and aromatic. Set aside.

3. Rinse quinoa in a fine mesh strainer until water runs clear, not cloudy. Combine quinoa, 2 ½ cups water, and chicken base in a small pot. Cover and bring to a boil. Turn heat down to low and simmer until water is completely absorbed, about 10-15 minutes. When done, quinoa will be soft and a white ring will pop out of the kernel. The white ring will appear only when it is fully cooked. Fluff with a fork. Set aside. A rice cooker may be used with the same quantity of quinoa, water, and chicken base.

4. Mix quinoa, onions, green chilies, and garlic in an 8" x 8" nonstick baking pan sprayed with nonstick cooking spray. Cover pan and bake at 350 °F for 40 minutes.

5. Toss in cilantro, green onions, pepitas, and optional lime juice to taste. Serve hot.

½ cup provides ⅛ cup vegetable and 1 ¼ oz equivalent grains.

Nutrients Per Serving: Calories **174**, Protein **6 g**, Carbohydrate **29 g**, Dietary Fiber **3 g**, Total Fat **4 g**, Saturated Fat **< 1 g**, Cholesterol **< 1 mg**, Vitamin A **244 IU (12 RAE)**, Vitamin C **10 mg**, Iron **2 mg**, Calcium **34 mg**, Sodium **93 mg**

Rainbow Rice

HIGHLAND ELEMENTARY SCHOOL
Cheshire, Connecticut

Our Story

Highland Elementary School is a dynamic and exciting place to work or to go to school. The recipe challenge team assembled and worked hard to create a recipe that was an instant smash hit. Rainbow Rice received great reviews during taste tests at the school.

Rainbow Rice is exactly that – a colorful rainbow of healthy vegetables, wholesome grains, and protein. Rainbow rice is certainly a wonderful way to introduce children to a variety of grains that they are sure to enjoy: brown rice, wild rice, barley, quinoa, and bulgur wheat. The team believes that once you have tasted "Rainbow Rice", you will feel like you've gone over the rainbow! Packed with whole grains and colorful vegetables, this recipe is a sure winner for those wanting a healthy dish without sacrificing taste.

School Team Members

SCHOOL NUTRITION PROFESSIONAL: Susan Zentek
CHEF: Patricia D'Alessio (Personal Chef, LLC)
COMMUNITY MEMBERS: Rebecca Frost (Teacher) and Katie Guerette (Teacher)
STUDENTS: Luke E., Randi C., Shane C., Maya G., and Jami P.

Rainbow Rice

Ingredients

½ cup Brown rice, long-grain, regular, dry

3 Tbsp Brown and wild rice blend, dry

6 Tbsp Barley, quick pearl, dry

2 tsp Low-sodium chicken base

2 Tbsp Quinoa, dry

3 Tbsp Bulgur wheat, dry

1 cup Fresh carrots, peeled, diced

1 cup Fresh red bell peppers, seeded, diced

1 tsp Extra virgin olive oil

¼ tsp Kosher salt

3 ½ cups Cooked diced chicken, ½" pieces (12 oz)

1 ½ cups Fresh baby spinach, chopped

Preparation Time: 15 minutes
Cooking Time: 1 hour
Makes six 1-cup servings

Directions

1. Preheat oven to 350 °F.

2. In a medium pot, combine brown rice, wild rice blend, barley, and 1 tsp chicken base with 1 ¼ cups water.

3. Rinse quinoa in a fine mesh strainer until water runs clear, not cloudy. In a small pot, combine quinoa and bulgur wheat with ¾ cup water and remaining 1 tsp chicken base.

4. Bring both uncovered pots to a rolling boil. Stir occasionally. Turn heat down and simmer over low heat until water is absorbed, about 30 minutes. Cover and cook an additional 10 minutes over low heat. Fluff with a fork.

5. In a large mixing bowl, combine carrots and red peppers. Drizzle with olive oil and sprinkle with salt. Toss lightly. Pour into a large nonstick baking pan. Roast at 350 °F for 20 minutes or until tender.

6. Combine cooked grains, chicken, and spinach with roasted vegetables. Mix well. Return to oven and bake for 15 minutes to an internal temperature of 165 °F or higher for at least 15 seconds (use a food thermometer to check the internal temperature). Serve hot.

1 cup provides 2 oz equivalent meat, ¼ cup vegetable and 1 oz equivalent grains.

Nutrients Per Serving: Calories **232**, Protein **22 g**, Carbohydrate **28 g**, Dietary Fiber **5 g**, Total Fat **4 g**, Saturated Fat **1 g**, Cholesterol **55 mg**, Vitamin A **5414 IU (271.09 RAE)**, Vitamin C **37 mg**, Iron **3 mg**, Calcium **29 mg**, Sodium **159 mg**

Stir-Fried Green Rice, Eggs, and Ham (Turkey Ham)

MCDOUGLE ELEMENTARY SCHOOL/CULBRETH MIDDLE SCHOOL
Chapel Hill, North Carolina

Our Story

A local restaurant owner and chef worked with the recipe challenge team comprised of students from McDougle Elementary School and Culbreth Middle School. The team developed this recipe using the chef's cooking style, consisting of North Carolina ingredients and Asian-inspired flavors. Stir-Fried Green Rice, Eggs, and Ham is a beautifully presented and colorful dish that will be an instant kids' favorite, not only due to the recipe's name, but also its taste!

School Team Members

SCHOOL NUTRITION PROFESSIONAL: Ryan McGuire
CHEF: Andrea Reusing (Owner, Lantern Restaurant)
COMMUNITY MEMBERS: Joe Palladino (Cafeteria Manager at Culbreth Middle School) and Liz Cartano (District Manager of the Food and Nutrition Department for Chapel Hill Carrboro City Schools)
STUDENT: Bridget P.

Whole Grains

Inspired by a popular children's book with a similar title, this hot main dish creatively combines brown rice, spinach, eggs, and turkey ham to create a great wholesome meal that satisfies the pickiest of eaters.

Stir-Fried Green Rice, Eggs, and Ham (Turkey Ham)

Ingredients

1 ¾ cups Brown rice, long-grain, regular, dry

⅓ tsp Salt

¾ cup Frozen chopped spinach, thawed, drained

6 large Whole eggs, beaten

1 Tbsp Vegetable oil

½ cup Extra-lean turkey ham, diced ¼" (2 oz)

¼ cup Fresh green onions, diced

1 tsp Sesame oil

1 tsp Low-sodium soy sauce

Preparation Time: 20 minutes
Cooking Time: 1 hour
Makes six 1-cup servings

Directions

1. Combine brown rice and 4 ½ cups water in a large pot and bring to a boil. Turn heat down to low. Cover and cook until water is absorbed, about 30-40 minutes. Fluff with a fork. Add salt to rice. Mix well. Set aside. A rice cooker may be used with the same quantity of brown rice and water.

2. Drain water from spinach by squeezing thawed spinach with hands. Set aside.

3. Whisk together eggs and 1 Tbsp water.

4. Cook half of the eggs in a large nonstick skillet coated with nonstick cooking spray. Remove eggs from skillet to cool. Chop cooled eggs and set aside. Reserve the remaining eggs for step 6.

5. Heat vegetable oil in a wok or a large nonstick skillet over high heat. Add ham and cook for 2 minutes or until ham begins to brown.

6. Reduce heat to medium. Add brown rice and toss to mix. Add remaining eggs. Stir for 5 minutes or until egg is fully cooked.

7. Add green onions, spinach, chopped egg, sesame oil, and soy sauce. Stir well. Cook until thoroughly heated. Serve hot.

1 cup provides 1 oz equivalent meat/meat alternate and 1 ½ oz equivalent grains.

Nutrients Per Serving: Calories **238,** Protein **9 g,** Carbohydrate **35 g,** Dietary Fiber **3 g,** Total Fat **7 g,** Saturated Fat **1 g,** Cholesterol **74 mg,** Vitamin A **1961 IU (120 RAE),** Vitamin C **< 1 mg,** Iron **1 mg,** Calcium **53 mg,** Sodium **313 mg**

Tasty Tots

BELLINGHAM MEMORIAL MIDDLE SCHOOL
Bellingham, Massachusetts

Our Story

The recipe challenge team at Bellingham Memorial Middle School began by brainstorming healthy menu items that would be well accepted by students. The team planned how to execute the contest's recipe development during an afterschool cooking class led by chefs from a Whole Foods Market. After a discussion on the value of healthy food and basic nutrition, the team divided into four groups and developed eight recipes.

The recipes were taste-tested by over 200 students and resulted in rave reviews. Two of these recipes, Tasty Tots and Mediterranean Quinoa Salad, became winning recipes featured in this cookbook.

Tasty Tots are a combination of sweet potatoes, garbanzo beans (chickpeas), and cinnamon that come together classically to form a unique, delicious side dish.

School Team Members

SCHOOL NUTRITION PROFESSIONAL: Jeanne Sheridan, SNS
CHEF: Rodney Poles (Whole Foods Market, partner chef from *Chefs Move to Schools* chefsmovetoschools.org)
COMMUNITY MEMBERS: Karen Ring (Healthy Eating Specialist, Whole Foods Market) and Lauren Marciszyn, RD, LDN (Youth and Community Wellness Director, YMCA)
STUDENTS: Dylan B., Elizabeth B., Taylin S., John G., and Nick D.

POPULAR CHOICE
Recipes for Healthy Kids

A healthy, kid-friendly alternative to traditional 'fried' potatoes, Tasty Tots are made with sweet potatoes and garbanzo beans (chickpeas).

Tasty Tots

Ingredients

5 cups Fresh sweet potatoes, peeled, coarsely shredded

2 ⅓ cups Canned low-sodium garbanzo beans (chickpeas), with liquid

½ cup Fresh green onions, finely chopped

2 Tbsp Vegetable oil

½ tsp Salt

½ tsp Granulated garlic

¼ tsp Ground black pepper

½ tsp Onion powder

½ tsp Ground cinnamon

Preparation Time: 30 minutes
Cooking Time: 35 minutes
Makes 36 Tots (serving size: 6 tots)

Directions

1. Preheat oven to 350 °F.

2. Place shredded potatoes on a large baking pan sprayed with a nonstick cooking spray. Bake at 350 °F for 20 minutes or until slightly tender. Do not overcook.

3. Increase oven temperature to 400 °F.

4. In a food processor or blender, purée garbanzo beans, including the liquid, until smooth.

5. In a medium mixing bowl, combine shredded sweet potatoes, puréed garbanzo beans, green onions, vegetable oil, salt, garlic, pepper, onion powder, and cinnamon. Mix well. Cover and refrigerate for 40-45 minutes to make tots easier to form.

6. Spray a large baking sheet with nonstick cooking spray. Using a cookie scoop or a spoon, roll 36 tots. Place 1 inch apart on baking sheet. Lightly flatten the tops of the tots with a spoon or a fork. Bake at 400 °F for 10-12 minutes or until lightly brown. Serve hot.

6 tots provide ¾ cup vegetable.*

*The legumes in this recipe contribute to the *vegetable component* and not the *meat/meat alternate component* since the beans are not visibly recognizable as legumes in the Tasty Tots recipe. This vegetable side dish with legumes is limited to the *vegetable component* because of its function as a vegetable in the meal.

Improving the nutrient content of the foods children eat by disguising nutrient-rich vegetables and fruits in the food is a great idea for people of all ages. However, it is not a menu planning principle that teaches and encourages children to recognize and choose a variety of healthy fruits and vegetables.

Nutrients Per Serving: Calories **172**, Protein **4 g**, Carbohydrate **28 g**, Dietary Fiber **5 g**, Total Fat **5 g**, Saturated Fat **0 g**, Cholesterol **0 mg**, Vitamin A **12609 IU (630 RAE)**, Vitamin C **13 mg**, Iron **1 mg**, Calcium **46 mg**, Sodium **377 mg**

Central Valley Harvest Bake

JOSHUA COWELL ELEMENTARY SCHOOL
Manteca, California

Our Story

The rich agricultural region of Manteca, California, grows many crops annually, including winter squash, pumpkin, corn, watermelon, and almonds. It was very important to the recipe team that they include locally grown produce in their recipe and introduce healthy, delicious vegetables to the students. Thus, butternut squash, a deep orange-colored winter squash with a sweet, nutty taste similar to pumpkin, was chosen as the featured vegetable of Central Valley Harvest Bake.

This succulent side dish combines the sweetness of butternut squash with the spicy kick of jalapenos and red peppers and is baked together with black beans, red quinoa, and granola for an absolutely delightful mouthful. It complements a variety of entrées, including grilled chicken or roast turkey.

School Team Members

SCHOOL NUTRITION PROFESSIONAL: Sandy Helsel
CHEF: Bryan Ehrenholm (Owner, Pure Joy Bakery and The Lunch Pail Restaurant)
COMMUNITY MEMBERS: Bonnie Bennett (School Principal) and Mary Tolan-Davi, RD (Community Registered Dietitian)
STUDENTS: Cameron H., Genesis M., Andrew R., Matthew M., and Elizabeth B.

1ST PLACE WINNER
Dark Green and Orange Vegetables

A succulent side dish that provides a striking contrast of flavors and textures.

Central Valley Harvest Bake

Ingredients

3 cups Fresh butternut squash, peeled, seeded, cubed ½"

2 tsp Extra virgin olive oil

⅓ cup Fresh red onions, peeled, diced

2 ¼ tsp Fresh jalapeno pepper, seeded, diced

¼ cup Fresh red bell pepper, seeded, diced

1 Tbsp Red quinoa, dry

¼ cup Canned low-sodium black beans, drained, rinsed

3 ½ tsp Fresh oregano, chopped

2 ½ Tbsp Sweetened applesauce

¼ tsp Kosher salt

2 Tbsp Fresh lime juice (optional)

¾ cup Low-fat granola, no fruit

Preparation Time: 45 minutes
Cooking Time: 1 hour 30 minutes
Makes six ½-cup servings

Directions

1. Preheat oven to 350 °F.

2. In a large bowl, toss squash in 1 tsp olive oil. Spread onto a large baking sheet sprayed with nonstick cooking spray. Roast in oven at 350 °F for 30 minutes or until tender and lightly brown around the edges. Remove and keep warm.

3. In a small bowl, toss onions, jalapeno peppers, and red peppers with remaining olive oil. Spread vegetables evenly onto a baking sheet sprayed with a nonstick cooking spray and roast in oven at 350 °F for 15 minutes or until tender and lightly brown around the edges. Check the vegetables often, they will brown very quickly. Remove and keep warm.

4. Rinse quinoa in a fine mesh strainer until water runs clear, not cloudy. Combine quinoa and ½ cup water in a small pot. Cover and bring to a boil. Turn heat down to low and simmer until water is completely absorbed, about 10-15 minutes. When done, quinoa will be soft and a white ring will pop out of the kernel. The white ring will appear only when it is fully cooked. Fluff with a fork. Set aside. A rice cooker may be used with the same quantity of quinoa and water.

5. In a large bowl, combine squash, black beans, quinoa, and oregano.

Nutrients Per Serving: Calories **97,** Protein **2 g,** Carbohydrate **20 g,** Dietary Fiber **4 g,** Total Fat **2 g,** Saturated Fat **< 1 g,** Cholesterol **0 mg,** Vitamin A **8912 IU (479 RAE),** Vitamin C **19 mg,** Iron **1 mg,** Calcium **44 mg,** Sodium **115 mg**

Directions for Central Valley Harvest Bake (continued)

6. Mix in applesauce, salt, and optional fresh lime juice.

7. Add onions, jalapeno peppers, and red peppers. Mix well.

8. Pour mixture into an 8" x 8" nonstick baking pan. Press gently to pack. Sprinkle granola evenly over the top of mixture. Bake for 30 minutes at 350 °F. Granola should be lightly browned. Serve hot.

½ cup provides ½ cup vegetable and ¼ oz equivalent grains.

Some Tips to Build a Healthy Meal

Dark Green and Orange Vegetables

From 10-Tips Nutrition Education Series

1. Make half your plate veggies and fruits

Vegetables and fruits are full of nutrients and may help to promote good health. Choose red, orange, and dark green vegetables such as tomatoes, sweet potatoes, and broccoli.

2. Include whole grains

Aim to make at least half your grains whole grains. Look for the words "100% whole grain" or "100% whole wheat" on the food label. Whole grains provide more nutrients, like fiber, than refined grains.

choosemyplate.gov/healthy-eating-tips/ten-tips.html

Stir-Fry Fajita Chicken, Squash, and Corn

MONUMENT VALLEY HIGH SCHOOL
Kayenta, Arizona

Our Story

On the Navajo Indian Reservation in Arizona, Monument Valley High School is part of the Kayenta Unified School District. For the recipe challenge, two student teams worked together to help prepare and sample dishes.

The team ultimately developed Stir-Fry Fajita Chicken, Squash, and Corn. This dish combines the sweet flavor of butternut squash with onions, corn, red peppers, and diced chilies brought together with a blend of spices and diced tomatoes. Stir-Fry Fajita Chicken, Squash, and Corn uses the natural flavors from vegetables and spices to make a savory meal, which can only be matched by the aroma produced when cooking.

School Team Members

SCHOOL NUTRITION PROFESSIONAL: Cathy Getz
CHEF: Paul Gray (Head Cook, Anasazi Inn)
COMMUNITY MEMBERS: Samantha J. Interpreter, RD, Lieutenant United States Public Health Service RDF-5 and Mike Williams
STUDENTS: Kevin B. and Brett B.

2ND PLACE WINNER
Dark Green and Orange Vegetables

This main dish creatively combines southwest spices with an Asian cooking style, blending the flavors of locally grown produce with fajita chicken strips, all stir-fried to perfection.

Stir-Fry Fajita Chicken, Squash, and Corn

Ingredients

1 ¾ cups Brown rice, long-grain, regular, dry

1 ½ tsp Salt-free chili-lime seasoning blend

¼ tsp Granulated garlic

1 Tbsp Fresh cilantro, chopped

2 Tbsp Canola oil

1 cup Fresh onions, peeled, diced

4 cups Cooked fajita chicken strips (16 oz)

3 ½ cups Fresh butternut squash, peeled, seeded, diced ½"

½ cup Fresh red bell peppers, seeded, diced

1 cup Frozen corn, thawed

½ cup Canned diced green chilies

½ cup Canned low-sodium diced tomatoes

½ tsp Ground black pepper

¾ tsp Ground cumin

¼ tsp Garlic powder

Preparation Time: 30 minutes
Cooking Time: 1 hour
Makes six ¾-cup servings stir-fry and six ½-cup servings brown rice

Directions

1. Combine brown rice and 4 ½ cups water in a large pot and bring to a rolling boil. Turn heat down to low. Cover and cook until water is absorbed, about 30-40 minutes. Sprinkle with ½ tsp salt-free seasoning blend, granulated garlic, and cilantro. Mix well. Keep warm. A rice cooker may be used with the same quantity of brown rice and water.

2. Heat canola oil in a large skillet or a wok. Cook onions for 2 minutes or until translucent.

3. Add chicken, squash, and remaining salt-free seasoning blend. Stir-fry over high heat for 10 minutes or until squash is tender.

4. Add red peppers, corn, green chilies, tomatoes, pepper, cumin, and garlic powder. Stir-fry over medium-high heat for no longer than 2 minutes so vegetables will remain crunchy. Do not overcook. Reduce heat to low and let simmer 2 minutes. Serve hot.

¾ cup stir-fry and ½ cup brown rice provides 1 ¼ oz equivalent meat, ¾ cup vegetable, and 1 oz equivalent grains.

Nutrients Per Serving: Calories **396,** Protein **20 g,** Carbohydrate **59 g,** Dietary Fiber **7 g,** Total Fat **10 g,** Saturated Fat **2 g,** Cholesterol **62 mg,** Vitamin A **7347 IU** **(359 RAE),** Vitamin C **44 mg,** Iron **2 mg,** Calcium **58 mg,** Sodium **574 mg**

Bok Choy Wrappers

WINOGRAD K-8 ELEMENTARY SCHOOL
Greeley, Colorado

Our Story

Students with a passion for food were handpicked by
their food science teacher. The culinary knowledge of
their school nutrition professional and a local chef, along
with the organizational skills of a community member,
rounded out this recipe challenge team. They combined
their love of food, clever personalities, and amazing
ideas to create a recipe students would enjoy.

The team used bok choy, a dark-green leafy Chinese
cabbage, a new vegetable for most students. They knew
that presentation would be the key in getting students
to try it.

This recipe challenged kids to try something new. Bok
Choy Wrappers are not your typical wrap! They let you
eat with your hands by making a wrap of crisp romaine
lettuce leaves filled with a delicious and nutritious
combination of chicken, pineapple, brown rice, and of
course, bok choy!

School Team Members

SCHOOL NUTRITION PROFESSIONAL: Kara Sample, RD, SNS
CHEF: Amanda Smith
COMMUNITY MEMBER: Emily Wigington (AmeriCorps
VISTA Volunteer)
STUDENTS: Jace K., Bethany V., Abraham A., and Amairani P.

Dark Green and Orange Vegetables

This dish offers a sweet
mixture of brown rice, juicy
pineapple, tasty chicken,
and bok choy, tossed with
sweet and sour sauce and
wrapped in a fresh, crisp
romaine lettuce leaf.

Bok Choy Wrappers

Ingredients

1 ½ cups Brown rice, long-grain, regular, dry

1 ¾ cups Fresh bok choy, sliced ¼"

1 ¾ cups Canned pineapple tidbits, in 100% juice

3 cups Cooked chicken strips (12 oz)

¾ cup Sweet and sour sauce

1 tsp Low-sodium soy sauce

12 leaves Fresh romaine lettuce, outer leaves

Preparation Time: 15 minutes
Cooking Time: 1 hour 15 minutes
Makes 12 wraps (two wraps per serving)

Directions

1. Preheat oven to 350 °F.

2. Combine brown rice and 3 ½ cups water in a large pot and bring to a rolling boil. Turn heat down to low. Cover and cook until water is absorbed, about 30-40 minutes. Fluff with a fork. A rice cooker may be used with the same quantity of brown rice and water.

3. In a medium bowl, combine brown rice, bok choy, pineapple, chicken, sweet and sour sauce, and soy sauce.

4. Transfer mixture to an 8" x 8" nonstick baking pan coated with nonstick cooking spray. Bake at 350 °F for 30 minutes. Cook to an internal temperature of 165 °F or higher for at least 15 seconds (use a food thermometer to check the internal temperature).

5. Place two lettuce leaves on a plate. Top each with ¾ cup filling. Optional: garnish with diced red peppers. Fold sides of lettuce in toward center; roll up like burrito. Place seam side down. Serve warm.

Note: Serving size may be too large for younger children and they may not be able to easily assemble the wrap. Filling may also be served over a bed of romaine lettuce.

2 wraps provide 1 oz equivalent meat, ¾ cup vegetable, ⅛ cup fruit, and 1 ½ oz equivalent grains.

1 wrap provides ½ oz equivalent meat, ⅜ cup vegetable, and ¾ oz equivalent grains.

Nutrients Per Serving (2 wraps): Calories **376**, Protein **13 g**, Carbohydrate **56 g**, Dietary Fiber **5 g**, Total Fat **11 g**, Saturated Fat **2 g**, Cholesterol **23 mg**, Vitamin A **4450 IU (224 RAE)**, Vitamin C **28 mg**, Iron **2 mg**, Calcium **71 mg**, Sodium **377 mg**

Crunchy Hawaiian Chicken Wrap

MOUNT LEBANON ELEMENTARY SCHOOL
Pendleton, South Carolina

Our Story

Mount Lebanon Elementary School is located in beautiful, historic Pendleton, South Carolina. For this competition, their "Healthy Kids Committee" worked diligently to develop, test, and prepare a recipe. The team tested the recipe and served it to a small group of students. To narrow down the choices, this wrap was cooked once with fish and once with chicken. The students were split half and half on which one they liked the best. The team chose chicken. Their creation, Crunchy Hawaiian Chicken Wrap, was so popular that it is currently featured on the Mount Lebanon Elementary School menu. As the name suggests, Crunchy Hawaiian Chicken Wrap is deliciously crunchy with a refreshing hint of tropical sweetness that kids find irresistible.

School Team Members

SCHOOL NUTRITION PROFESSIONAL: Vikki Mullinax
CHEF: Lorett Arnold-Hayes (Owner and Chef, 1826 On The Green)
COMMUNITY MEMBER: Kristi Martin (School Nurse)
STUDENT: Chandler W.

Dark Green and Orange Vegetables

This appealing main dish combines seasoned chicken, sweet pineapple, and crunchy shredded vegetables, topped with a delicious poppy seed dressing all wrapped in a warm, whole-wheat tortilla.

Crunchy Hawaiian Chicken Wrap

Ingredients

¼ cup Light mayonnaise

⅛ cup White vinegar

¼ cup Sugar

1 tsp Poppy seeds

1 ½ tsp Garlic powder

1 ½ tsp Onion powder

1 ½ tsp Chili powder

2 cups Fresh broccoli, shredded

1 ½ cups Fresh carrots, peeled, shredded

¼ cup Canned crushed pineapple, in 100% juice, drained

1 cup Fresh baby spinach, chopped

3 cups Cooked diced chicken, ½" pieces (12 oz)

6 Whole-wheat tortillas, 10"

Preparation Time: 20 minutes
Makes six wraps

Directions

1. In a small mixing bowl, combine mayonnaise, vinegar, sugar, poppy seeds, garlic powder, onion powder, and chili powder for the dressing. Mix well. Cover and refrigerate.

2. Combine broccoli, carrots, pineapple, and spinach in a large bowl. Stir in dressing and chicken. Mix well. Serve immediately or cover and refrigerate.

3. For each wrap, place ⅔ cup filling on the bottom half of the tortilla and roll in the form of a burrito. Place seam side down. Cut diagonally. Serve immediately.

Suggestion
Filling may be made up to one day in advance. Assemble wraps when ready to serve.

1 wrap (two halves) provides 2 oz equivalent meat, ½ cup vegetable, and 1 ¾ oz equivalent grains.

½ wrap (one half) provides 1 oz equivalent meat, ¼ cup vegetable, and ¾ oz equivalent grains.

Nutrients Per Serving (1 wrap): Calories **308**, Protein **24 g**, Carbohydrate **42 g**, Dietary Fiber **5 g**, Total Fat **6 g**, Saturated Fat **2 g**, Cholesterol **53 mg**, Vitamin A **3845 IU (193 RAE)**, Vitamin C **27 mg**, Iron **4 mg**, Calcium **83 mg**, Sodium **408 mg**

Harvest Delight

THE PROTESTANT GUILD FOR HUMAN SERVICES, INC.
Waltham, Massachusetts

Our Story

The recipe challenge team was formed when the students at The Guild expressed an interest in learning how to cook healthier, fresher meals. To meet this need, the Harvest Delight dish was created. It features locally grown ingredients seasoned with fresh aromatic herbs and a subtle taste of maple. It was served to the entire student body who were requested to complete an evaluation form. Over 90 percent of the students who evaluated the recipe rated it "very good" to "excellent." The team was overjoyed with the recipe's positive feedback. Who knew that sweet potatoes, butternut squash, carrots, spinach, dried cranberries, and apples could cause so much excitement? Your kids will be happy too when they taste this colorful and delicious blend of vegetables, fruits, and herbs.

School Team Members

SCHOOL NUTRITION PROFESSIONAL: Doreen Mangini, PhD
CHEF: Chef Florentine
COMMUNITY MEMBER: Erin Ridge (Special Education Teacher)
STUDENT: Samantha I.

Dark Green and Orange Vegetables

Inspired by autumn vegetables found at farmers markets, Harvest Delight is an irresistible, brilliantly colored roasted vegetable and fruit medley side dish.

Harvest Delight

Ingredients

1 ⅓ cups Fresh green apples, peeled, cored, diced ½"

⅓ cup Fresh carrots, peeled, sliced ¼"

1 cup Fresh sweet potatoes, peeled, cubed 1"

1 cup Fresh butternut squash, peeled, seeded, cubed ½"

⅓ cup Fresh red onions, peeled, diced

2 Tbsp Extra virgin olive oil

¼ tsp Sea salt

1 tsp Fresh thyme, chopped

1 tsp Fresh oregano, chopped

1 tsp Fresh sage, chopped

1 tsp Fresh rosemary, chopped

1 tsp Fresh garlic, minced

2 ½ tsp Maple syrup

1 cup Fresh baby spinach, chopped

⅛ cup Dried cranberries, finely chopped

Preparation Time: 30-40 minutes
Cooking Time: 1 hour
Makes six ½-cup servings

Directions

1. Preheat oven to 425 °F.

2. You may place diced apples in a small bowl of water with a squirt of lemon juice to prevent them from browning. Drain when ready to use.

3. Steam carrots in a steam basket over high heat for 10 minutes or until soft.

4. Toss potatoes, squash, carrots, and red onions in a large mixing bowl with olive oil and salt.

5. Line a large baking pan with parchment paper and spray with nonstick cooking spray. Spread vegetables evenly on baking pan. Roast vegetables in oven at 425 °F for 25 minutes or until tender and slightly browned. Turn vegetables once midway through roasting.

6. In a large mixing bowl, combine apples, thyme, oregano, sage, rosemary, and garlic.

7. Remove vegetables from oven, lower heat to 400 °F. Add apple mixture to vegetables. Spread evenly. Return to the oven and roast for 15 minutes or until slightly tender.

8. Remove from oven. Drizzle with maple syrup and mix well. Return to oven. Roast for 8 additional minutes at 400 °F until vegetables are fork-tender.

Nutrients Per Serving: Calories **93,** Protein **1 g,** Carbohydrate **16 g,** Dietary Fiber **3 g,** Total Fat **3 g,** Saturated Fat **0 g,** Cholesterol **0 mg,** Vitamin A **11204 IU (560 RAE),** Vitamin C **11 mg,** Iron **2 mg,** Calcium **38 mg,** Sodium **103 mg**

Directions for Harvest Delight (continued)

9. Remove vegetables from the oven and gently toss in spinach. Mix in cranberries. Serve hot.

½ cup provides ½ cup vegetable and ⅛ cup fruit.

Dark Green and Orange Vegetables

From 10-Tips Nutrition Education Series

1. Add lean protein
Choose protein foods, such as lean beef and pork, or chicken, turkey, beans, or tofu. Twice a week, make seafood the protein on your plate.

2. Don't forget the dairy
Pair your meal with a cup of fat-free or low-fat milk. They provide the same amount of calcium and other essential nutrients as whole milk, but less fat and calories. Don't drink milk? Try soymilk (soy beverage) as your beverage or include fat-free or low-fat yogurt in your meal.

3. Avoid extra fat
Using heavy gravies or sauces will add fat and calories to otherwise healthy choices. For example, steamed broccoli is great, but avoid topping it with cheese sauce. Try other options, like a sprinkling of low-fat parmesan cheese or a squeeze of lemon.

choosemyplate.gov/healthy-eating-tips/ten-tips.html

Roasted Fish Crispy Slaw Wrap

LIBERTY MIDDLE SCHOOL
Orlando, Florida

Our Story

There are many benefits to living in Orlando, Florida. Liberty Middle School realized this when they learned a local chef from Universal Studios would be a member on their recipe challenge team. At the initial meeting, the chef discussed the importance of healthy food choices and introduced new ingredients, including bok choy which was used in their recipe creation.

The recipe also used whole-wheat tortillas, meeting the need to offer more whole grains in kids' diets. With the school's kitchen staff, the recipe challenge team developed the Roasted Fish Crispy Slaw Wrap. The team is ecstatic to have their recipe featured in this cookbook and is sure that other children will enjoy this crunchy, tasty delight!

School Team Members

SCHOOL NUTRITION PROFESSIONAL: Sharon Springer
CHEF: Ed Colleran (Executive Sous Chef, Universal Studios)
COMMUNITY MEMBER: Sarah Thornquest (Physical Education Teacher)
STUDENTS: Joshua A., Tyler W., Kimberly A., Shalima D., and Priscilla R.

Dark Green and Orange Vegetables

A combination of colors and textures that overflows with fresh vegetables, spicy fish, and a burst of citrus, all contained in a whole-wheat tortilla, with fresh avocado.

Roasted Fish Crispy Slaw Wrap

Ingredients

2 ½ cups Fresh red cabbage, shredded

2 cups Fresh white cabbage, shredded

1 ½ cups Fresh carrots, peeled, shredded

1 cup Fresh bok choy, julienne cut "shoestring strips" ⅛"

2 Tbsp Fresh cilantro, chopped

¾ cup Low-fat balsamic vinaigrette dressing

1 Tbsp Salt-free chili-lime seasoning blend

1 Tbsp Extra virgin olive oil

6 Tilapia fish filets, raw, 4 oz each

1 ½ cup Fresh romaine lettuce, julienne cut "shoestring strips" ⅛"

6 Whole-wheat tortillas, 8"

6 slices Fresh avocado, peeled, pitted, sliced

6 quarters Fresh limes, quartered

Preparation Time: 50 minutes
Cooking Time: 12 minutes
Makes six wraps

Directions

1. Preheat oven to 375 °F.

2. In a large mixing bowl combine red and white cabbages, carrots, bok choy, cilantro, and balsamic dressing to make the slaw. Cover and refrigerate for at least 1 hour.

3. Place fish filets on a baking sheet lined with parchment paper sprayed with nonstick cooking spray. Brush fish with olive oil and sprinkle with salt-free seasoning blend. Roast uncovered at 375 °F for 12 minutes or until internal temperature reaches 145 °F or higher and fish flakes with a fork. Use a food thermometer to check the internal temperature.

4. Remove fish from oven.

5. To assemble wrap: Place ¼ cup lettuce on tortilla. Cut fish in half and place both pieces on top of lettuce. Add 1 cup cabbage slaw and a slice of avocado. Squeeze lime on top of mixture. Roll in the form of a burrito. Cut diagonally. Serve immediately.

1 wrap (two halves) provides 2 ¾ oz equivalent meat, 1 ⅜ cup vegetable, and 1 ½ oz equivalent grains.

½ wrap (one half) provides 1 ¼ oz equivalent meat, ⅝ cup vegetable, and ¾ oz equivalent grains.

Nutrients Per Serving (1 wrap): Calories **342**, Protein **29 g**, Carbohydrate **37 g**, Dietary Fiber **6 g**, Total Fat **10 g**, Saturated Fat **2 g**, Cholesterol **50 mg**, Vitamin A **6406 IU (350 RAE)**, Vitamin C **47 mg**, Iron **3 mg**, Calcium **69 mg**, Sodium **541 mg**

Smokin' Powerhouse Chili

WEST JUNIOR HIGH SCHOOL
Minnetonka, Minnesota

Our Story

The recipe challenge team developed dishes that were prepared by school nutrition staff and offered to students during their lunch hour. Taste test results showed that Smokin' Powerhouse Chili was a success! This dish stands apart because of its warm, rich flavors.

As the recipe challenge team describes it, Smokin' Powerhouse Chili is "the bomb!" It is the healthiest and tastiest chili you'll ever eat! As a main dish, it has a smoky blend of spices and some of Minnesota's best harvest to warm you up from the inside out on a cold winter's day!

School Team Members

SCHOOL NUTRITION PROFESSIONAL: Barbara Mechura
CHEF: Jenny Breen, MS (Co-owner, Good Life Catering)
COMMUNITY MEMBERS: Mary Jo Martin (Parent and School Nurse) and Sue Nefzger (Parent and Family and Consumer Science Teacher)
STUDENTS: Ryan K., Liam P., Ty L., Miranda H., and Matt H.

Dark Green and Orange Vegetables

A chili made of a blend of vegetables, black beans, and smoky spices all served with ancient Aztec whole-grain quinoa.

Smokin' Powerhouse Chili

Ingredients

⅔ cup Quinoa, dry

1 cup Fresh onion, peeled, diced

2 tsp Fresh garlic, minced

¾ cup Low-sodium vegetable stock

1 ¼ cups Fresh carrots, peeled, diced ½"

½ cup Fresh red bell peppers, seeded, diced

½ tsp Ground chipotle pepper (optional)

1 cup Fresh sweet potatoes, peeled, diced ½"

1 ¾ cups Canned low-sodium diced tomatoes

1 cup Canned low-sodium tomato sauce

¼ cup Fresh cilantro, chopped

2 ½ tsp Chili powder

2 ½ tsp Ground cumin

¼ tsp Salt

2 cups Canned low-sodium black beans, drained, rinsed

½ cup Frozen corn

Preparation Time: 30 minutes
Cooking Time: 1 hour 25 minutes
Makes six 1-cup servings chili and six ¼-cup servings quinoa

Directions

1. Rinse quinoa in a fine mesh strainer until water runs clear, not cloudy. Combine quinoa and 1 ⅓ cups water in a small pot. Cover and bring to a boil. Turn heat down to low and simmer uncovered until water is completely absorbed, about 10-15 minutes. When done, quinoa will be soft and a white ring will pop out of the kernel. The white ring will appear only when it is fully cooked. Fluff with a fork and set aside. A rice cooker may be used with the same quantity of quinoa and water.

2. In a large pot coated with nonstick cooking spray, cook onions and garlic over low-medium heat for 2 minutes. Add half of the vegetable stock and bring to a boil.

3. Add carrots, red bell pepper, and optional ground chipotle pepper. Cook uncovered over medium heat for 10 minutes.

4. Steam sweet potatoes in a steam basket over high heat. Cover and steam for 15 minutes or until fork-tender.

5. Add remaining vegetable stock to pot along with diced tomatoes, tomato sauce, cilantro, chili powder, cumin, and salt. Cook uncovered over medium heat, stirring occasionally, allowing mixture to thicken and flavors to blend for about 15 minutes.

6. Add black beans, corn, and steamed sweet potatoes. Cover and continue cooking over low heat for 10-15 minutes.

Nutrients Per Serving: Calories **184**, Protein **7 g**, Carbohydrate **38 g**, Dietary Fiber **8 g**, Total Fat **2 g**, Saturated Fat **< 1 g**, Cholesterol **0 mg**, Vitamin A **9024 IU (435 RAE)**, Vitamin C **39 mg**, Iron **3 mg**, Calcium **63 mg**, Sodium **256 mg**

Directions for Smokin' Powerhouse Chili (continued)

7. Serve ¼ cup quinoa with 1 cup chili. Serve hot.

May serve brown rice in place of quinoa.

---

1 cup chili and ¼ cup quinoa provides:

Legume as Meat Alternate: ½ oz equivalent meat alternate, 1 cup vegetable, and ½ oz equivalent grains.

OR

Legume as Vegetable: 1 ⅛ cup vegetable and ½ oz equivalent grains.

Legume vegetable can be counted as either a meat alternate or as a legume vegetable but not as both simultaneously.

Tips for Affordable Fruits and Veggies

Dark Green and Orange Vegetables

From 10-Tips Nutrition Education Series

1. Celebrate the season
Use fresh vegetables and fruits that are in season. They are easy to get, have more flavor, and are usually less expensive. Your local farmers market is a great source of seasonal produce.

2. Why pay full price?
Check the local newspaper, online, and at the store for sales, coupons, and specials that will cut food costs. Often, you can get more for less by visiting larger grocery stores (discount grocers if available).

3. Stick to your list
Plan out your meals ahead of time and make a grocery list. You will save money by buying only what you need. Don't shop when you're hungry. Shopping after eating will make it easier to pass on the tempting snack foods. You'll have more of your food budget for vegetables and fruits.

choosemyplate.gov/healthy-eating-tips/ten-tips.html

Squish Squash Lasagna

LIBERTY ELEMENTARY SCHOOL
Powell, Ohio

Our Story

The team from Liberty Elementary School wanted to create a tasty recipe that would be enjoyed by kids. They started the recipe development process by sending survey questions to students in 4th and 5th grades. With feedback from students, they developed Squish Squash Lasagna. This tantalizing dish features butternut squash, a deep orange-colored winter squash with a sweet, nutty taste similar to pumpkin that children are sure to enjoy. After sampling the Squish Squash Lasagna recipe, many students returned for second helpings. That's when the team knew that the Squish Squash Lasagna recipe was a hit. Give your kids some excitement by serving this mouthwatering main dish at mealtime!

School Team Members

SCHOOL NUTRITION PROFESSIONAL: Jackie Billman
CHEF: Jeff Lindemeyer (Executive Chef, Cameron Mitchell Restaurants)
COMMUNITY MEMBERS: Nicole Hancock and Michelle Lounsbury
STUDENTS: Tori L., Alexis H., Leah L., and Buddy F.

Dark Green and Orange Vegetables

This savory recipe is made with a slightly sweet tomato sauce deliciously tucked between layers of whole-wheat lasagna noodles, butternut squash, and spinach, all nestled under part-skim mozzarella cheese.

Squish Squash Lasagna

Ingredients

¼ tsp Canola oil

¾ cup Fresh onions, peeled, diced

2 tsp Fresh garlic, minced

1 ½ cups Canned low-sodium diced tomatoes

¼ tsp Dried oregano

¼ tsp Dried thyme

¼ tsp Dried basil

8 Whole-wheat lasagna sheets, no-boil, 3 ½" x 7" sheets

1 ¼ cups Fresh spinach, julienne cut "shoestring strips" ⅛"

22 slices Fresh butternut squash, peeled, seeded, sliced ¼" (1 medium)

¾ cup Low-fat mozzarella cheese, low moisture, part skim, shredded (3 oz)

Preparation Time: 30 minutes
Cooking Time: 1 hour 35 minutes
Makes six servings

Directions

1. Preheat oven to 350 °F.

2. Heat canola oil in a medium pot over medium-high heat. Add onions, and garlic. Cook for 2-3 minutes or until tender. Add tomatoes, oregano, thyme, and basil. Reduce heat to low and simmer, uncovered, for 30 minutes, stirring occasionally. Add ½ cup water. Mix well.

3. Divide sauce into 3 equal parts (about ¾ cup each) and set aside for step 6.

4. Place pasta sheets in a bowl filled with hot water for 5 minutes. Remove sheets as needed to assemble lasagna.

5. Spray bottom and sides of an 8" x 8" nonstick baking pan with nonstick cooking spray.

6. To Assemble:
   a. Place 4 lasagna sheets overlapping, covering the bottom of the pan
   b. Cover evenly with about ¾ cup tomato sauce
   c. Spread half of the spinach (about ¾ cup) evenly over sauce
   d. Place 11 slices of squash on top of spinach, slightly overlapping
   e. Repeat layering steps a-d
   f. Cover with remaining sauce (about ¾ cup)

Cover tightly with aluminum foil and bake at 350 °F for 50 minutes or until squash is fork-tender.

Nutrients Per Serving: Calories **175,** Protein **8 g,** Carbohydrate **29 g,** Dietary Fiber **5 g,** Total Fat **4 g,** Saturated Fat **2 g,** Cholesterol **8 mg,** Vitamin A **9103 IU (456 RAE),** Vitamin C **18 mg,** Iron **1 mg,** Calcium **149 mg,** Sodium **83 mg**

Directions for Squish Squash Lasagna (continued)

7. Remove lasagna from oven. Sprinkle cheese evenly over top.

8. Bake uncovered for 5 minutes or until cheese melts and browns slightly.

9. Remove lasagna from oven and allow to rest for 15 minutes before serving.

10. Cut into 6 even pieces. Serve hot.

One piece provides ½ oz equivalent meat alternate, ¾ cup vegetable, and ¾ oz equivalent grains.

From 10-Tips Nutrition Education Series

1. Try canned or frozen

Compare the price and the number of servings from fresh, canned, and frozen forms of the same veggie or fruit. Canned and frozen items may be less expensive than fresh. For canned items, choose fruit canned in 100% fruit juice and vegetables with "low sodium" or "no salt added" on the label.

2. Buy small amounts frequently

Some fresh vegetables and fruits don't last long. Buy small amounts more often to ensure you can eat the foods without throwing any away.

choosemyplate.gov/healthy-eating-tips/ten-tips.html

Sweet Potato and Black Bean Stew

SKYLINE HIGH SCHOOL
Oakland, California

Our Story

Skyline High School is located at the crest of the Oakland Hills in California. The team grew out of an existing afterschool cooking academy that teaches cooking skills and nutrition. The team is excited to have their recipe, Sweet Potato and Black Bean Stew, represented in this cookbook.

Sweet Potato and Black Bean Stew was created when the team at Skyline High School decided to match an unlikely pair of ingredients. The wonderful recipe combination is as savory as it is sweet. This stew is brought to a healthy and earthy conclusion with flavorful Swiss chard, a delicate and mild-flavored, dark-green leafy vegetable. Served over brown rice or whole-wheat couscous, this stew warms the soul and feeds the mind.

School Team Members

SCHOOL NUTRITION PROFESSIONAL: Donnie Barclift
CHEF: Jenny Huston
COMMUNITY MEMBERS: Rusty Hopewell (Health Center Nutritionist) and Sage Moore
STUDENTS: Karen M., Quailyn S., and Rudy R.

Dark Green and Orange Vegetables

This hearty main dish combines the sweetness of orange sweet potatoes and the robustness of black beans, with the surprise addition of Swiss chard and a light touch of cumin. Serve over brown rice or whole-wheat couscous for a warm delight!

Sweet Potato and Black Bean Stew

Ingredients

2 Tbsp Vegetable oil

½ small pepper Dried New Mexican chili pepper, whole

1 ¼ cups Fresh onions, peeled, diced

1 tsp Ground cumin

1 ½ cups Fresh sweet potatoes, peeled, cubed ½"

6 cups Canned low-sodium black beans, drained, rinsed

¾ cup Orange juice

1 cup Low-sodium chicken stock

1 Tbsp Red wine vinegar

¼ tsp Salt

¼ tsp Ground black pepper

4 cups Fresh Swiss chard, no stems, chopped

Preparation Time: 20 minutes
Cooking Time: 40 minutes
Makes six 1-cup servings

Directions

1. Heat vegetable oil in a large pot. Cook chili pepper and onions for 1-2 minutes.

2. Add cumin and cook for 2 minutes..

3. Add sweet potatoes, black beans, orange juice, and chicken stock. Bring to a boil. Cover and reduce heat to low. Simmer for 20 minutes or until the potatoes are tender.

4. Remove chili pepper and discard.

5. Add vinegar, salt, and pepper.

6. Add Swiss chard. Cover and continue cooking until Swiss chard is tender. Serve hot.

May serve over brown rice or whole-wheat couscous.

1 cup provides:

Legume as Meat Alternate: 3 oz equivalent meat alternate and ½ cup vegetable.

 OR

Legume as Vegetable: 1 ¼ cup vegetable.

Legume vegetable can be counted as either a meat alternate or as a legume vegetable but not as both simultaneously.

Nutrients Per Serving: Calories **222,** Protein **10 g,** Carbohydrate **43 g,** Dietary Fiber **12 g,** Total Fat **4 g,** Saturated Fat **< 1 g,** Cholesterol **0 mg,** Vitamin A **8848 IU (442 RAE),** Vitamin C **26 mg,** Iron **4 mg,** Calcium **103 mg,** Sodium **536 mg**

Tuscan Smoked Turkey and Bean Soup

IRA B. JONES ELEMENTARY SCHOOL
Asheville, North Carolina

Our Story

Asheville, North Carolina is known for its heritage, arts, and fine dining. Ira B. Jones Elementary School in Asheville shares a taste of another well-known region of fine dining–Tuscany–as its recipe team prepared Tuscan Smoked Turkey and Bean Soup. The team worked together to develop the recipe, and a number of students tasted and evaluated the recipe before it was submitted.

The team's hard work paid off! The recipe features Navy beans, which are actually white in color, but got their popular name because they were a staple food of the U.S. Navy in the early 20th century. Tuscan Smoked Turkey and Bean Soup is sure to tease and please the senses and warm the toes! Delizioso!!

School Team Members

SCHOOL NUTRITION PROFESSIONAL: Susan Bowers
CHEF: Denny Trantham (Executive Chef, The Grove Park Inn, Resort and Spa)
COMMUNITY MEMBERS: Tara Jardine (Volunteer Coordinator and Representative, AmeriCorps) and Sarah Cain (Principal)
STUDENT: Nichelle B.

1ST PLACE WINNER
Dry Beans and Peas

This hearty soup will surely tantalize taste buds with tender smoked turkey chunks, Navy beans, and a colorful array of veggies, all simmered in a deliciously seasoned broth.

Ingredients

⅓ cup Fresh onions, peeled, diced ½"

⅓ cup Fresh celery, diced

⅓ cup Fresh carrots, peeled, diced

1 ½ cups Fresh kale, no stems, chopped

2 ¼ tsp Canned low-sodium tomato paste

1 Tbsp Fresh garlic, minced

4 ¼ cups Low-sodium chicken stock

1 ¾ cups Canned low-sodium Navy beans, drained, rinsed

½ tsp Salt

⅛ tsp Ground black pepper

1 cup Smoked turkey breast, ¼" pieces (5 oz)

2 tsp Fresh thyme, chopped

2 tsp Fresh basil, chopped

2 tsp Fresh parsley, chopped

Preparation Time: 30 minutes
Cooking Time: 50 minutes
Makes six 1-cup servings

Directions

1. Place onions, celery, carrots, kale, tomato paste, and garlic in a large pot coated with nonstick cooking spray. Cook over medium-high heat. Stir frequently. Cook until vegetables are softened and onions are translucent.

2. Add chicken stock, beans, salt, and pepper.

3. Reduce temperature to low heat. Cover and simmer for 20 minutes. Stir occasionally.

4. Add turkey, thyme, basil, and parsley. Stir well. Simmer a minimum of 10 minutes. Serve hot.

1 cup provides:

Legume as Meat Alternate: 1 ½ oz equivalent meat/meat alternate and ¼ cup vegetable.

OR

Legume as Vegetable: ½ oz equivalent meat and ½ cup vegetable.

Legume vegetable can be counted as either a meat alternate or as a legume vegetable but not as both simultaneously.

Nutrients Per Serving: Calories **135**, Protein **15 g**, Carbohydrate **14 g**, Dietary Fiber **4 g**, Total Fat **3 g**, Saturated Fat **<1 g**, Cholesterol **21 mg**, Vitamin A **3058 IU (153 RAE)**, Vitamin C **7 mg**, Iron **2 mg**, Calcium **62 mg**, Sodium **525 mg**

Lentils of the Southwest

SWEENEY ELEMENTARY SCHOOL
Santa Fe, New Mexico

Our Story

With the support of Cooking with Kids, a nonprofit organization in Santa Fe that provides hands-on nutrition education each year to elementary school students in public schools, the Sweeney Elementary School recipe challenge team came together to create this delicious dish.

Lentils have so much potential for meals. Packed with protein, vitamins, and fiber, they are easy to cook and have great versatility. Lentils of the Southwest can be served as a side dish to make the perfect New Mexican lunch. When accompanied by brown rice, this lentil recipe becomes a tasty main dish. The team is very happy that their recipe was chosen as a winner to be represented in the cookbook.

School Team Members

SCHOOL NUTRITION PROFESSIONAL: Judi Jacquez (Director, Student Nutrition Services)
CHEF: Rocky Durham
COMMUNITY MEMBERS: Jane Stacey (Program Director, Cooking with Kids) and Anna Farrier (Community Liaison, Cooking with Kids)
STUDENTS: Melanie S., Jailey B., Marisol B., Diana O., and Nicole A.

2ND PLACE WINNER
Dry Beans and Peas

Flavored with ground red chili, cumin, garlic, and a touch of tomatoes, these lentils have a "salsa flavor" that kids are sure to love.

Ingredients

½ cup Lentils, green or brown, dry

1 tsp Extra virgin olive oil

2 Tbsp Fresh onions, peeled, diced

1 tsp Fresh garlic, minced

1 tsp Ground cumin

1 tsp Ground red chili pepper

½ tsp Chili powder

½ cup Canned low-sodium diced tomatoes

½ tsp Salt

2 Tbsp Fresh cilantro, chopped

Preparation Time: 15 minutes
Cooking Time: 50 minutes
Makes six ¼-cup servings

Directions

1. In a small pot, combine the lentils and 1 ¼ cups water. Bring to a boil over high heat. Reduce the heat to low and cook uncovered until tender, about 30 minutes.

2. Heat olive oil in a medium skillet. Add onions and garlic. Cook for 3-5 minutes or until tender. Stir in cumin, red chili pepper, and chili powder. Reduce heat to low and cook for 2 minutes.

3. Add onion/garlic mixture to cooked lentils. Add ¼ cup plus 2 tablespoons water. Stir in tomatoes and salt. Bring to a boil over high heat. Reduce heat to low and simmer, uncovered, for 20 minutes.

4. Just before serving stir in cilantro. Serve hot.

¼ cup provides:

Legume as Meat Alternate: 1 oz equivalent meat alternate.
OR
Legume as Vegetable: ¼ cup vegetable.

Legume vegetable can be counted as either a meat alternate or as a legume vegetable but not as both simultaneously.

Nutrients Per Serving: Calories **69**, Protein **5 g**, Carbohydrate **11 g**, Dietary Fiber **4 g**, Total Fat **< 1 g**, Saturated Fat **< 1 g**, Cholesterol **0 mg**, Vitamin A **251 IU (10 RAE)**, Vitamin C **3 mg**, Iron **2 mg**, Calcium **15 mg**, Sodium **142 mg**

Confetti Soup

BURKE MIDDLE AND HIGH SCHOOL
Charleston, South Carolina

Our Story

Located in Charleston, South Carolina, Burke Middle and High School takes pride in sharing its rich history. The school strives to help each student reach his/her individual potential while achieving measurable success in the classroom.

This recipe challenge team formed a dynamic group with a local restaurant chef as their lead. The chef invited the team members to his restaurant to begin developing recipes for the competition. They worked to perfect the recipes and later prepared the recipes for the students to try. All of their hard work resulted in Confetti Soup. This isn't your everyday soup—your kids will surely be asking for more!

School Team Members

SCHOOL NUTRITION PROFESSIONAL: Erin Boudolf, RD
CHEF: Craig Deihl
COMMUNITY MEMBERS: Jennifer Moore (The Medical University of South Carolina's Boeing Center for Promotion of Healthy Lifestyles in Children and Families) and Coleen Martin (The Medical University of South Carolina's Boeing Center for Promotion of Healthy Lifestyles in Children and Families)
STUDENTS: Auja R., Keshawn J., Quatifah L., and Tyler M.

Dry Beans and Peas

This delicious recipe mixes together black-eyed peas, savory smoked turkey ham, fresh vegetables, and a secret ingredient, kale, to make up this warm, winter-wonder soup!

Confetti Soup

Ingredients

1 ¾ tsp Canola oil

¾ cup Fresh onions, peeled, diced

¾ cup Fresh celery, diced

¾ cup Fresh carrots, peeled, diced

½ tsp Salt

½ tsp Ground black pepper

¼ tsp Whole fennel seed

⅛ tsp Crushed red pepper (optional)

1 ½ cups Canned low-sodium black-eyed peas, drained, rinsed

3 ½ cups Water

1 cup Extra-lean turkey ham, diced ¼" (6 oz)

⅓ cup Fresh kale, coarsely chopped

1 ½ Tbsp Fresh parsley, chopped

Preparation Time: 20 minutes
Cooking Time: 40 minutes
Makes six 1-cup servings

Directions

1. In a large pot, heat oil over medium-high heat. Add onions and celery. Cook for 2-3 minutes or until tender. Add carrots, salt, pepper, fennel seed, and optional crushed red pepper. Cook for an additional 2-3 minutes.

2. Add black-eyed peas and water. Cook uncovered for 25 minutes over medium heat.

3. Add turkey ham and kale. Cook covered for an additional 10 minutes over medium heat until kale is tender.

4. Add parsley right before serving. Serve hot.

1 cup provides:

Legume as Meat Alternate: 1 ½ oz equivalent meat/meat alternate and ¼ cup vegetable.
OR
Legume as Vegetable: ½ oz equivalent meat and ½ cup vegetable.

Legume vegetable can be counted as either a meat alternate or as a legume vegetable but not as both simultaneously.

Nutrients Per Serving: Calories **94,** Protein **8 g,** Carbohydrate **10 g,** Dietary Fiber **3 g,** Total Fat **3 g,** Saturated Fat **< 1 g,** Cholesterol **18 mg,** Vitamin A **3033 IU (152 RAE),** Vitamin C **4 mg,** Iron **1 mg,** Calcium **35 mg,** Sodium **488 mg**

Eagle Pizza

BYARS ELEMENTARY SCHOOL
Byars, Oklahoma

Our Story

Byars Elementary School is located approximately an hour southeast of Oklahoma City. It is one of the few pre-kindergarten through 8th grade schools in the State. The recipe challenge team decided to name their creation after the school mascot. Members of the community teamed up with the school to pursue the challenge with Eagle Pride! Taste-tested by the student body, Eagle Pizza was a winner.

Eagle Pizza will give kids the power and energy they need for a busy day. This versatile recipe can easily be made with help from the kids. Eagle Pizza is a tasty choice that will make your sense of pride soar like an eagle when they smile over this yummy combination of pizza and taco!

School Team Members

SCHOOL NUTRITION PROFESSIONAL: Vickie Spray
CHEF: Ruth Burrows, DTR
COMMUNITY MEMBER: Sandra Walck (past School Board Member)
STUDENTS: Gracie S., Braden P., Shawn M., Shawn T., and Travis W.

Dry Beans and Peas

A delicious combination of pizza and taco, this recipe is made with whole-grain tostada shells, refried beans, shredded cheese, and a stack of colorful veggies.

Eagle Pizza

Ingredients

½ cup Fresh spinach, julienne cut "shoestring strips"

½ cup Fresh romaine lettuce, julienne cut "shoestring strips"

2 ¼ tsp Salt-free chili-lime seasoning blend*

1 ¾ cups Canned low-sodium refried beans, fat-free

¾ cup Fresh green bell pepper, seeded, diced

¾ cup Fresh onions, peeled, diced

1 ¼ cups Canned low-sodium corn, drained, rinsed

6 Whole-grain tostada shells

6 Tbsp Reduced-fat Mexican cheese blend, shredded (1 ½ oz)

1 cup Fresh carrots, peeled, shredded

½ cup Low-sodium salsa, mild

½ cup Fat-free sour cream

Preparation Time: 25 minutes
Cooking Time: 10 minutes
Makes six Tostada Pizzas

Directions

1. Preheat oven to 350 °F.

2. Combine spinach and lettuce in bowl and set aside.

3. In a medium mixing bowl, combine salt-free seasoning blend and refried beans. Set aside.

4. In a small skillet, coated with nonstick cooking spray, cook green peppers, onions, and corn for 3-4 minutes. Set aside.

5. For each pizza, place ¼ cup of bean filling on tostada shell. Spread mixture evenly using the back of a spoon. Top with ⅓ cup sautéed vegetable mixture. Lightly sprinkle 1 Tbsp of cheese on top.

6. Place tostadas on a large baking sheet coated with nonstick cooking spray. Bake until cheese is melted, about 2 minutes.

7. Remove tostadas from oven. Top each tostada with:
  About 1 Tbsp spinach/lettuce mixture
  About 2 ½ Tbsp carrots
  About 1 Tbsp salsa
  About 1 Tbsp sour cream

  Serve immediately.

Nutrients Per Serving: Calories **206**, Protein **9 g,** Carbohydrate **32 g,** Dietary Fiber **6 g,** Total Fat **6 g,** Saturated Fat **2 g,** Cholesterol **7 mg,** Vitamin A **3227 IU (177 RAE),** Vitamin C **20 mg,** Iron **2 mg,** Calcium **173 mg,** Sodium **290 mg**

Directions for Eagle Pizza (continued)

*If desired, use 2 ¼ tsp Salt-Free Taco Seasoning Blend in place of salt-free chili-lime seasoning.

Salt-Free Taco Seasoning Blend

1 tsp dried onion

1 tsp chili powder

½ tsp ground cumin

½ tsp crushed red pepper

½ tsp garlic powder

¼ tsp oregano

½ tsp cornstarch

Combine all ingredients. If using immediately do not add cornstarch. Store in an airtight container.

1 tostada pizza provides:

Legume as Meat Alternate: 1 ¼ oz equivalent meat alternate, ¾ cup vegetable, and ½ oz equivalent grains.

OR

Legume as Vegetable: ¼ oz equivalent meat alternate, 1 cup vegetable, and ½ oz equivalent grains.

Legume vegetable can be counted as either a meat alternate or as a legume vegetable but not as both simultaneously.

More Tips to Build a Healthy Meal

From 10-Tips Nutrition Education Series

1. Take your time
Savor your food. Eat slowly, enjoy the taste and textures, and pay attention to how you feel. Be mindful. Eating very quickly may cause you to eat too much.

2. Try new foods
Keep it interesting by picking out new foods you've never tried before, like mango, lentils, or kale. You may find a new favorite! Trade fun and tasty recipes with friends or find them online.

choosemyplate.gov/healthy-eating-tips/ten-tips.html

Fiesta Mexican Lasagna

ITHACA CITY SCHOOL DISTRICT
Ithaca, New York

Our Story

At the Ithaca City School District in picturesque Ithaca in upstate New York, their mission is to educate every student to become a life-long learner. The team's chef is a co-owner of a local restaurant which is considered one of the "pioneer" restaurants for preparing and serving healthy, local, plant-based meals.

For its entry in the *Recipes for Healthy Kids* Competition, the team worked to create Fiesta Mexican Lasagna and conducted numerous taste tests with students. This hearty main dish features golden butternut squash, corn, and peppers roasted until sweet and the natural flavors caramelize together. This deliciously spicy spin on an Italian classic will leave your kids wanting more!

School Team Members

SCHOOL NUTRITION PROFESSIONAL: Denise Agati (Food Service Director)
CHEF: Wynnie Stein (Chef, Moosewood Restaurant)
COMMUNITY MEMBERS: Amie Hamlin (Executive Director, New York Coalition for Healthy School Food) and Eric Smith (Owner, Cayuga Pure Organics)
STUDENTS: Alyia C. and Josie W. (Middle School Students)

Dry Beans and Peas

This main dish is filled with hearty, healthy ingredients. It's colorful vegetables are layered with crunchy tortilla chips, smooth black beans, flavorful cumin, oregano, and lively salsa, and baked to perfection as an aromatic, savory casserole.

Fiesta Mexican Lasagna

Ingredients

66 chips Low-sodium tortilla chips (about 12 oz)

2 tsp Canola oil

¼ cup Fresh green bell pepper, seeded, diced

1 cup Canned low-sodium corn, drained, rinsed

1 cup Fresh onions, peeled, diced

2 cups Fresh butternut squash, peeled, seeded, cubed ½"

½ tsp Ground oregano

½ tsp Ground cumin

½ tsp Granulated garlic

½ tsp Chili powder

½ tsp Paprika

½ tsp Salt

2 ½ cups Canned low-sodium black beans, drained, rinsed

1 ¼ cups Low-sodium meatless spaghetti sauce

1 cup Low-sodium salsa, mild

Preparation Time: 30 minutes
Cooking Time: 60 minutes
Makes six servings

Directions

1. Preheat oven to 350 °F.

2. Divide chips evenly into three bowls (about 22 chips per bowl). Crumble one bowl of chips and reserve remaining two bowls of whole chips for use during the layering process.

3. In a medium mixing bowl, combine canola oil, green pepper, corn, and ½ cup of onions, reserving other half of onions for step 6. Toss to evenly coat with oil. Transfer vegetables to a large baking sheet. Roast uncovered at 350 °F for 15 minutes or until vegetables are slightly brown around the edges.

4. Steam squash in a steam basket over high heat for 15 minutes or until soft. Place squash in a large mixing bowl and mash until smooth.

5. Add roasted vegetables to squash. Mix well. Add ¼ teaspoon oregano and ¼ teaspoon cumin, reserving remaining spices for step 6. Mix well and set aside.

6. In a medium skillet coated with nonstick cooking spray, cook remaining onions, cumin, and oregano with garlic, chili powder, paprika, and salt over medium heat for 5 minutes or until the onions become translucent and soft.

7. Purée cooked onions and black beans in a food processor or blender until smooth. If needed, add 1-2 tablespoons of water to make the purée smoother.

Nutrients Per Serving: Calories **264,** Protein **9 g,** Carbohydrate **52 g,** Dietary Fiber **9 g,** Total Fat **4 g,** Saturated Fat **< 1 g,** Cholesterol **1 mg,** Vitamin A **3769 IU (180 RAE),** Vitamin C **16 mg,** Iron **2 mg,** Calcium **120 mg,** Sodium **425 mg**

Directions for Fiesta Mexican Lasagna (continued)

8. To make the sauce, combine spaghetti sauce and salsa in a bowl and set aside.

9. Layer ingredients in an 8" x 8" nonstick baking pan sprayed with nonstick spray.
  a. 1 cup sauce
  b. Bowl of whole chips (about 22 whole chips)
  c. 1 ¼ cups bean mixture (a rubber spatula dipped in water helps to spread the mixture evenly)
  d. 1 ⅛ cups squash/vegetable mixture
  e. Bowl of whole chips (about 22 whole chips)
  f. 1 ¼ cups bean mixture
  g. 1 ⅛ cups squash/vegetable mixture
  h. 1 ¼ cups sauce
  i. Bowl of crumbled chips

10. Cover with aluminum foil and bake at 350 °F for 30 minutes until thoroughly heated.

11. Remove from oven. Uncover and allow to rest for 15 minutes before serving.

12. Cut into six even portions. Serve hot.

One piece provides:

Legume as Meat Alternate: 1 oz equivalent meat alternate, ¾ cup vegetable, and ¾ oz equivalent grains.

OR

Legume as Vegetable: 1 cup vegetable and ¾ oz equivalent grains.

Legume vegetable can be counted as either a meat alternate or as a legume vegetable but not as both simultaneously.

More Tips to Build a Healthy Meal

Dry Beans and Peas

From 10-Tips Nutrition Education Series

1. Use a smaller plate
Use a smaller plate at meals to help with portion control. That way you can finish your entire plate and feel satisfied without overeating.

2. Take control of your food
Eat at home more often so you know exactly what you are eating. If you eat out, check and compare the nutrition information. Choose healthier options such as baked instead of fried.

3. Satisfy your sweet tooth in a healthy way
Indulge in a naturally sweet dessert dish—fruit! Serve a fresh a or a fruit parfait made with yogurt. For a hot dessert, bake apples and top with cinnamon.

choosemyplate.gov/healthy-eating-tips/ten-tips.html

Fiesta Wrap

CHARTER OAK INTERNATIONAL ACADEMY
West Hartford, Connecticut

Our Story

Charter Oak International Academy, nestled in the midst of the West Hartford, Connecticut School District, is a thriving magnet school with students from 20 countries, speaking 14 languages! For the contest the recipe challenge team included students from three schools involved in the *Chefs Move to Schools* program or *Farm to School* pilot program and one of the founders of "Growing Great Schools," a newly formed parent advocacy group. Their winning creation, Fiesta Wrap, combines spices, whole grains, legumes, and vibrant vegetables to create a taste that is unforgettable. To top it off, kids can crown their wraps with fresh tomatoes, lettuce, and corn salsa.

School Team Members

SCHOOL NUTRITION PROFESSIONAL: Sharon Riley (Area Manager, School Nutrition Services)
CHEF: Hunter Morton (Executive Chef, Max's Downtown Restaurant)
COMMUNITY MEMBER: Alicia Brown (Parent)
STUDENTS: Cole C., Sasha W., Remie H., Noa B., and Niranda M.

Dry Beans and Peas

This delicious main dish features a quinoa and black bean filling seasoned with spices, lime juice, and a medley of carrots, red peppers, red onions, and reduced-fat cheddar cheese.

Fiesta Wrap

Ingredients

¼ cup Quinoa, dry

2 ¼ cups Canned low-sodium black beans, drained, rinsed

¼ cup Fresh red bell pepper, seeded, diced

¼ cup Fresh red onions, peeled, diced

½ cup Fresh carrots, peeled, shredded

¼ cup Reduced-fat white cheddar cheese, shredded (1 oz)

1 tsp Chili powder

1 ¼ tsp Ground cumin

1 ¼ tsp Fresh Lime juice

6 Whole-wheat tortillas, 6"

1 Tbsp Vegetable oil

Preparation Time: 15 minutes
Cooking Time: 25 minutes
Makes six wraps

Directions

1. Preheat oven to 325 °F.

2. Rinse quinoa in a fine mesh strainer until water runs clear, not cloudy. Combine quinoa and ¾ cup water in a small pot. Cover and bring to a boil. Turn heat down to low and simmer until water is completely absorbed, about 10-15 minutes. When done, quinoa will be soft and a white ring will pop out of the kernel. The white ring will appear only when it is fully cooked. Fluff with a fork and set aside. A rice cooker may be used with the same quantity of quinoa and water.

3. Place black beans in a large mixing bowl. Lightly mash beans by squeezing them using gloved hands (at least 50 percent of the beans should appear whole). Be careful not to over-mash beans.

4. To make filling, add to the mashed beans the quinoa, red peppers, red onions, carrots, cheese, chili powder, cumin, and lime juice.

5. For each wrap, place ½ cup of filling on the bottom half of tortilla and roll in the form of a burrito.

The wrap may also be folded in half like a taco.

6. Brush filled wraps lightly with vegetable oil and place on a baking sheet. Bake for 10 minutes at 325 °F. Wraps will be lightly brown. Serve hot.

Nutrients Per Serving: Calories **175**, Protein **7 g**, Carbohydrate **27 g**, Dietary Fiber **5 g**, Total Fat **5 g**, Saturated Fat **< 1 g**, Cholesterol **2 mg**, Vitamin A **1465 IU (77 RAE)**, Vitamin C **12 mg**, Iron **2 mg**, Calcium **62 mg**, Sodium **346 mg**

Directions for Fiesta Wrap (continued)

If desired, serve with fresh diced tomatoes, corn salsa, and/or lettuce.

1 wrap provides:

Legume as Meat Alternate: 1 oz equivalent meat alternate and 1 oz equivalent grains.

OR

Legume as Vegetable: ¼ cup vegetable and 1 oz equivalent grains.

Legume vegetable can be counted as either a meat alternate or as a legume vegetable but not as both simultaneously.

More Tips for Affordable Fruits and Veggies

Dry Beans and Peas

From 10-Tips Nutrition Education Series

1. Buy in bulk when items are on sale

For fresh vegetables or fruits you use often, a large size bag is the better buy. Canned or frozen fruits or vegetables can be bought in large quantitites when they are on sale, since they last much longer.

2. Store brands = savings

Opt for store brands when possible. You will get the same or similar product for a cheaper price. If your grocery store has a membership card, sign up for even more savings.

3. Keep it simple

Buy vegetables and fruits in their simplest form. Pre-cut, pre-washed, ready-to eat, and processed foods are convenient, but often cost much more than when purchased in their basic forms.

choosemyplate.gov/healthy-eating-tips/ten-tips.html

Harvest Stew

DAVID D. JONES ELEMENTARY SCHOOL
Greensboro, North Carolina

Our Story

When the recipe challenge team came together to work on this project, they had no idea what they had gotten themselves into. Their first task was figuring out how to organize a tasting event because their school had over 750 students. The team then experimented with different ingredients and recipes which led to the development of Harvest Stew. The school is proud that North Carolina sweet potatoes from their *Farm to School* program were used in this stew.

This flavorful dish was created to satisfy the palate, while being a filling, nutritious meal to fuel the body for the rest of the day. Kids will be ecstatic over the taste of this recipe.

School Team Members

SCHOOL NUTRITION PROFESSIONAL: Pam Cecil
CHEF: Matthias Hartmann
COMMUNITY MEMBERS: Jen Schell (Parent) and Amanda Hester (Nutritionist)
STUDENTS: Maria S., Bailey P., Nemiah I., Jalen W., and Ayatollah H.

Dry Beans and Peas

This hearty dish is a perfect blend of spinach, sweet potatoes, red potatoes, northern beans, tomatoes, and chicken. To round out the dish, the flavors of carrots, celery, onions, and garlic take this stew to the next level!

Harvest Stew

Ingredients

¾ Tbsp Vegetable oil

¾ cup Fresh onions, peeled, diced

⅓ cup Fresh carrots, peeled, diced

½ cup Fresh celery, diced

1 Tbsp Enriched all-purpose flour

⅓ tsp Low-sodium chicken base

1 ¼ cups Water

⅛ tsp Salt-free seasoning

⅓ tsp Garlic powder

1 cup Canned low-sodium diced tomatoes

1 cup Fresh sweet potatoes, peeled, cubed 1"

½ cup Fresh red potato, unpeeled, cubed 1"

1 cup Cooked diced chicken, ½" pieces (3 oz)

2 cups Canned low-sodium great northern beans, drained, rinsed

½ cup Fresh baby spinach, chopped

Preparation Time: 40 minutes
Cooking Time: 30-40 minutes
Makes six ¾-cup servings

Directions

1. Heat vegetable oil in a large pot over medium heat. Cook onions, carrots, and celery for 5 minutes allowing them to brown slightly.

2. Sprinkle flour over the vegetables. Stir well. Add chicken base and water. Stir constantly. Bring to a boil.

3. Reduce heat to medium. Stir in salt-free seasoning and garlic powder. Cook uncovered for 2 minutes. Add tomatoes, sweet potatoes, and red potatoes. Simmer uncovered for 15 minutes or until potatoes are tender. Stir frequently. Add chicken, beans, and spinach. Stir.

4. Continue to simmer uncovered for 10 minutes. Serve hot.

¾ cup provides:

Legume as Meat Alternate: 1 ½ oz equivalent meat/meat alternate and ⅜ cup vegetable.

OR

Legume as Vegetable: ½ oz equivalent meat and ⅝ cup vegetable.

Legume vegetable can be counted as either a meat alternate or as a legume vegetable but not as both simultaneously.

Nutrients Per Serving: Calories **124**, Protein **8 g**, Carbohydrate **18 g**, Dietary Fiber **5 g**, Total Fat **2 g**, Saturated Fat **< 1 g**, Cholesterol **13 mg**, Vitamin A **3426 IU (163 RAE)**, Vitamin C **9 g**, Iron **2 mg**, Calcium **50 mg**, Sodium **57 mg**

Purple Power Bean Wrap

NEWMAN ELEMENTARY SCHOOL
Needham, Massachusetts

Dry Beans and Peas

Rolled up in a whole-wheat tortilla are avocado, white beans, lettuce, and shredded purple cabbage that pack a powerful purple punch in this delicious vegetarian wrap.

Our Story

Newman Elementary School is the largest elementary school in the Needham Public School District. It serves over 700 students in preschool through the 5th grade, offering an engaging and supportive learning environment to all of the students.

The recipe competition was a great opportunity for the students to play a major role in sustaining a healthy school environment. Six students were able to participate on the recipe challenge team, which worked for several weeks trying different recipes that combined puréed beans with a variety of different ingredients.

The team eventually decided that avocado and purple cabbage yielded the best color and flavor combination. Their end result was an entrée called Purple Power Bean Wrap—a delicious, nutritious, and really cool vegetarian meal. It is sure to surprise and delight your children!

School Team Members

SCHOOL NUTRITION PROFESSIONAL: Steve Farrell
CHEF: Sue Findlay
COMMUNITY MEMBERS: Kim Benner (Parent) and Anne Hayek (Parent)
STUDENTS: James B., John B., Maeve B., Sophie F-W., Becca S., and Chloé M.

Purple Power Bean Wrap

Ingredients

1 tsp Lemon zest (make zest from juiced lemon)

2 Tbsp Fresh lemon, juiced

2 cups Canned low-sodium great northern beans, drained, rinsed

½ cup Fresh avocado, peeled, pitted, puréed

1 Tbsp Fresh garlic, minced

2 ¼ tsp Extra virgin olive oil

⅓ tsp Chili powder

½ tsp Salt

1 ½ cups Fresh purple cabbage, finely shredded

6 Whole-wheat tortillas, 10"

3 cups Fresh romaine lettuce, shredded

Preparation Time: 20 minutes
Cooking Time: 20 minutes
Makes six wraps

Directions

1. Grate lemon rind on hand-held grater or citrus zester to make zest. Juice lemons. Set aside.

2. Purée beans in a food processor or a blender until smooth. Put into a large mixing bowl and set aside.

3. Purée avocado, lemon juice, lemon zest, garlic, olive oil, chili powder, and salt until smooth. Mix into pureed beans. Add shredded cabbage. Mix well.

4. You may cover and refrigerate at 40 °F for no more than 2 hours to avoid browning of avocado.

5. For each wrap, place ⅓ cup of bean filling on the bottom half of tortilla. Top with ½ cup of lettuce. Roll in the form of a burrito. Cut diagonally. Serve immediately.

1 wrap (two halves) provides:

Legume as Meat Alternate: ½ oz equivalent meat alternate, ⅝ cup vegetable, and 1 ¾ oz equivalent grains.

OR

Legume as Vegetable: ¾ cup vegetable and 1 ¾ oz equivalent grains.

½ wrap (one half) provides:

⅜ cup vegetable and ¾ oz equivalent grains.

Legume vegetable can be counted as either a meat alternate or as a legume vegetable but not as both simultaneously.

Nutrients Per Serving (1 wrap): Calories274, Protein **8 g,** Carbohydrate **38 g,** Dietary Fiber **8 g,** Total Fat **10 g,** Saturated Fat **< 1 g,** Cholesterol **0 mg,** Vitamin A **2880 IU (144 RAE),** Vitamin C **24 mg,** Iron **2 mg,** Calcium **54 mg,** Sodium **424 mg**

Spanish Chickpea Stew

SKYLINE HIGH SCHOOL
Oakland, California

Our Story

Skyline High School is located on a beautiful 45-acre campus at the crest of the Oakland Hills in California. The recipe challenge team grew out of an existing afterschool cooking academy that teaches cooking skills and nutrition. After conducting taste tests and receiving approvals by the students, the team eventually submitted not one, but two stew recipes which were selected to be featured in this cookbook: Spanish Chickpea Stew and Sweet Potato and Black Bean Stew.

The hearty Spanish Chickpea Stew will make a delightful addition to your menu. The flavors of this stew are well-balanced by the slight acidity of the tomatoes, creating a delicious main dish when served over brown rice or whole-wheat couscous.

School Team Members

SCHOOL NUTRITION PROFESSIONAL: Donnie Barclift
CHEF: Jenny Huston
COMMUNITY MEMBERS: Rusty Hopewell (Health Center Nutritionist) and Sage Moore
STUDENTS: Karen M., Quailyn S., and Rudy R.

Dry Beans and Peas

The mild spicing of cumin and paprika, the heartiness of chickpeas, the soothing taste of spinach, the slight acidity of tomatoes, and the sweetness of golden raisins, create a delicious stew that will make your mouth water.

Spanish Chickpea Stew

Ingredients

3 Tbsp Extra virgin olive oil

2 tsp Fresh garlic, minced

2 cups Fresh onions, peeled, diced

2 tsp Sweet paprika

½ tsp Ground cumin

3 cups Frozen spinach, chopped

2 cups Canned low-sodium garbanzo beans (chickpeas), drained, rinsed

¾ cup Golden raisins

1 cup Canned low-sodium diced tomatoes

1 ½ cups Low-sodium chicken stock

1 Tbsp Red wine vinegar

¼ tsp Salt

¼ tsp Ground black pepper

Preparation Time: 15 minutes
Cooking Time: 20-25 minutes
Makes six 1-cup servings

Directions

1. In a large pot, heat olive oil over medium heat.

2. Add garlic and cook for 1 minute. Add onions and continue to cook for 2-3 minutes until onions are translucent.

3. Mix in paprika and cumin.

4. Add spinach and cook for 7 minutes.

5. Add garbanzo beans (chickpeas), raisins, tomatoes, and chicken stock. Bring to a boil.

6. Reduce heat to low and simmer uncovered for 7-10 minutes, or until raisins are plump.

7. Add vinegar, salt, and pepper. Mix well. Serve hot.

1 cup provides:

Legume as Meat Alternate: 1 ½ oz equivalent meat alternate, ⅜ cup vegetable, and ¼ cup fruit.

OR

Legume as Vegetable: ¾ cup vegetable and ¼ cup fruit.

Legume vegetable can be counted as either a meat alternate or as a legume vegetable but not as both simultaneously.

Nutrients Per Serving: Calories **241**, Protein **8 g**, Carbohydrate **38 g**, Dietary Fiber **6 g**, Total Fat **8 g**, Saturated Fat **1 g**, Cholesterol **0 mg**, Vitamin A **3325 IU (159 RAE)**, Vitamin C **7 mg**, Iron **2 mg**, Calcium **93 mg**, Sodium **156 mg**

Vegetable Chili Boat

CEDAR CLIFF HIGH SCHOOL
Camp Hill, Pennsylvania

Our Story

Cedar Cliff High School is committed to preparing students to be responsible adults. The school seized the competition as an opportunity to involve students, parents, and community members in a real-life challenge of creating a nutritious recipe kids enjoy.

The recipe team, which included a chef, a student team member, and the school nutrition professional, created the Vegetable Chili Boat recipe. It was selected by over 250 students, and survey results indicated the majority of the students would purchase it again. This recipe packs a punch with southwest flavor! It is a delight to the eye and a fiesta for the mouth!

School Team Members

SCHOOL NUTRITION PROFESSIONAL: Todd Stoltz
CHEF: Thomas Long, CEC AAC (Executive Chef, Sodexo at Holy Spirit Hospital)
COMMUNITY MEMBER: Jaci Scott (Family and Consumer Science Teacher)
STUDENT: Tessa L.

Dry Beans and Peas

This warm and wonderful vegetarian chili will light up your palate with three flavorful beans mixed together with vegetables and spices, surrounded by crunchy corn tortilla chips, and sprinkled with a blend of cheeses.

Vegetable Chili Boat

Ingredients

2 ½ tsp Canola oil

½ cup Fresh onion, peeled, diced

½ cup Fresh green bell pepper, seeded, diced

½ cup Canned low-sodium pinto beans, drained, rinsed

½ cup Canned low-sodium kidney beans, drained, rinsed

1 cup Canned low-sodium black beans, drained, rinsed

1 ½ Tbsp Chili powder

1 ⅓ cups Canned low-sodium diced tomatoes

1 cup Low-sodium chicken stock

1 dash Hot sauce

¼ cup Canned low-sodium tomato paste

18 chips Low-sodium tortilla chips (about 3 oz)

¼ cup Reduced-fat cheddar cheese, shredded (1 oz)

¼ cup Low-fat mozzarella cheese, low moisture, part skim, shredded (1 oz)

Preparation Time: 20 minutes
Cooking Time: 25 minutes
Makes six ¾-cup servings

Directions

1. Heat canola oil in a large pot over medium-high heat. Add onions and green peppers. Cook for 2-3 minutes or until tender. Add beans and stir to coat. Add chili powder. Stir. Cook for 1 minute for flavors to blend.

2. Add tomatoes, chicken stock, and hot sauce. Bring to a boil. Simmer uncovered for 10 minutes. Add tomato paste and mix well. Cook uncovered for an additional 10 minutes. Bring to a rolling boil for at least 15 seconds. Reduce heat to low and simmer to keep warm.

3. Combine cheddar and mozzarella cheeses (the cheese is a garnish).

4. Place ¾ cup chili in a bowl. Top with 3 chips and sprinkle with about 1 tablespoon of cheese blend. Serve hot.

¾ cup provides:

Legume as Meat Alternate: ¾ oz equivalent meat alternate, ⅜ cup vegetable, and ¼ oz equivalent grains.

OR

Legume as Vegetable: ¼ oz equivalent meat alternate, ½ cup vegetable, and ¼ oz equivalent grains.

Legume vegetable can be counted as either a meat alternate or as a legume vegetable but not as both simultaneously.

Nutrients Per Serving: Calories **141**, Protein **7 g,** Carbohydrate **21 g,** Dietary Fiber **5 g,** Total Fat **4 g,** Saturated Fat **1 g,** Cholesterol **4 mg,** Vitamin A **1226 IU (64 RAE),** Vitamin C **14 mg,** Iron **2 mg,** Calcium **118 mg,** Sodium **159 mg**

Conversion Charts

METRIC AND IMPERIAL CONVERSIONS

(These conversions are rounded for convenience)

Ingredient	Cups/Table-spoons/Teaspoons	Ounces	Grams/Milliliters
Butter	1 cup/ 16 tablespoons/ 2 sticks	8 ounces	230 grams
Cheese, shredded	1 cup	4 ounces	110 grams
Cream cheese	1 tablespoon	0.5 ounce	14.5 grams
Cornstarch	1 tablespoon	0.3 ounce	8 grams
Flour, all-purpose	1 cup/1 tablespoon	4.5 ounces/0.3 ounce	125 grams/8 grams
Flour, whole wheat	1 cup	4 ounces	120 grams
Fruit, dried	1 cup	4 ounces	120 grams
Fruits or veggies, chopped	1 cup	5 to 7 ounces	145 to 200 grams
Fruits or veggies, pureed	1 cup	8.5 ounces	245 grams
Honey, maple syrup, or corn syrup	1 tablespoon	0.75 ounce	20 grams
Liquids: cream, milk, water, or juice	1 cup	8 fluid ounces	240 milliliters
Oats	1 cup	5.5 ounces	150 grams
Salt	1 teaspoon	0.2 ounce	6 grams
Spices: cinnamon, cloves, ginger, or nutmeg (ground)	1 teaspoon	0.2 ounce	5 milliliters
Sugar, brown, firmly packed	1 cup	7 ounces	200 grams
Sugar, white	1 cup/1 tablespoon	7 ounces/0.5 ounce	200 grams/12.5 grams
Vanilla extract	1 teaspoon	0.2 ounce	4 grams

OVEN TEMPERATURES

Fahrenheit	Celsius	Gas Mark
225°	110°	¼
250°	120°	½
275°	140°	1
300°	150°	2
325°	160°	3
350°	180°	4
375°	190°	5
400°	200°	6
425°	220°	7
450°	230°	8

Index

Notes

Notes